Closer to Heaven

Ten Principles to Grow your Wings and Create Heaven on Earth

Corry Lang

Authentic Life Publishing
P.O. Box 231824
Encinitas, CA 92023

Closer to Heaven
Ten Principles to grow your Wings
and create Heaven on Earth

Cover design: Prudence Makhura

Printed in the United States of America
First Printing 2019
First Edition 2019

ISBN 978-1-7339368-1-1

10 9 8 7 6 5 4 3 2 1

Praise for "Closer to Heaven"

"Ms Lang provides a how-to guide for Creating Heaven on Earth by incorporating her Ten Principles into an easy-to read novella. Ben's story portrays our own flaws that cause our suffering and self-defeating behaviors. Ben's angel, Daniel, provides him (and the reader) effective cognitive and behavioral strategies all with a strong spiritual underpinning. Closer to Heaven is worth years of therapy."

Thomas A. Flanagan, M.D., board certified Psychiatrist, Associate Clinical Professor of Psychiatry, UCSD, former Medical Director, Aurora Behavioral Health Care, Distinguished Fellow of the American Psychiatric Association

"Corry Lang's book, **Closer to Heaven**, *takes the reader on a journey revealing the secrets of living a joyful life. She provides the reader with principles that will enable one to grow their innate wings and create heaven on Earth. In a wholistic manner she explores both attitudes towards oneself and attitudes towards the environment. These include non-violence, truthfulness, non-stealing, fidelity, non-coveting, purification, contentment, and dedication to the Divine. In a most intriguing and entertaining way, this book presents the fictional life of a person as they experience the depths of despair that life*

may present all the way to the bliss of a life well-lived. How and why form the basis of the book with insights and practices as well. The book is well worth reading, highly recommended."

John Grimes, Ph.D., Professor of Indian Studies and Philosophy, Researcher, Author of thirteen books, primarily on Advaita Vedanta (school of Hindu Philosophy and one of the classic Indian paths to spiritual realization).

"Corry Lang's book compelled me to become more impeccable in my word – the words I say to myself and to others - particularly the words I use concerning awareness, mindfulness and compassion. This is her first book, and one that will warm the hearts of the many people who seek more meaning in their lives and guidance for pursuing it.. Here's to observing and noticing . . . what we miss and what we add on to our moment-to-moment experiences of life, whether on a trail in the woods or in a city café. Read it—it's a page-turner—and you will evolve. Yes, you ***can*** *"empty", start anew, and* ***create*** *something you never imagined!"*

Patricia Robinson, PhD, Psychologist, Worldwide trainer for psychologists, social workers, physicians, nurses and health coaches. Author of *Brief Interventions for Radical Change* and the *Mindfulness and Acceptance Workbook for Depression.*

"Corry Lang's writing is like listening to a friend who just got back from an enlightening journey. As they tell you about their experiences, you somehow grow with them throughout their story. "Closer to Heaven" rings a bell of familiarity that makes you feel related and vulnerable to the characters and their perspectives. As you read along, you'll find yourself applying the principles in this book noticing how your awareness, your attachments, and how present you can be, construct the fabric of your reality. This book is an entertaining tool for the soul to recognize itself in your story. It helped me to be more aware of things, of being present, or not being attached. Thank you for sharing it with me. It's a great book! And it's something that's applicable and useful in people's lives."

Adam Turner, Video Designer & Production Supervisor

"Corry Lang's first novel "Closer to Heaven" is based on her own yoga practices and life coaching principles. She outlines ten rules that will help you live a more balanced and peaceful life. Her book is thought provoking and inspiring. Corry outlines her principles in an enjoyable story of a downtrodden man who succeeds to turn his life around."

Andrea Harris, Qualcomm San Diego Manager/Senior Staff

"I really liked the relationship between the two male friends. There was love and intimacy and connection and this could be empowering for our communities in the way that men relate to one another. It was a simple yet gentle process. There is one principle per chapter, emotionally relatable, and they can be applied to life. Each chapter is complete and they also build on each other to create a whole bigger picture. I felt that reading this book was an opportunity of seeing into another's way of being. It was inviting, accepting, not preaching at all, but tolerant and non-judgmental. Corry Lang isn't trying to convert, but inclusive and tolerant. For people who are new to this (higher consciousness) reading this book could be a gentle and comprehensive way to help shift the masculine, patriarchal perspective. It's a great read!"

Shannon Ward, Reiki Master and massage therapist, Professional singer/songwriter, Performer, Vocal healer and Coach

"Wow! The first chapter instantly drew me in! Great writing, great story!! Corry Lang presents ten powerful lessons that really add a deeper perspective to the human experience all wrapped up in a light, fun, fast-moving narrative that is easy to absorb. The two main characters are relatable and well developed as the reader hears their thoughts, listens to their conversations, and views their interactions as they move through the ten lessons that Daniel must complete

in order to "earn his wings back" and return to heaven. However, it is Ben who truly grows the most.

Taking her readers in and out of many different real life settings over the course of a week, the author's descriptions create the space and time for us to visually become immersed in the experience as Ben learns to apply each principle, proving that when we are open to change, it really can be that easy."

Elizabeth DeHaas, High School teacher,
B.A. English Literature

Table of Contents

1. Ben

It was late at night when Ben got off the freeway. It had been another strenuous sales meeting in a faraway city. He wondered how much longer he would be able to do this. He was becoming less and less sure about the effectiveness and safety of his company's product and he was tired of offering it to the world.

He took his foot off the gas pedal and approached the stop light at the end of the off-ramp. The flight had been fine; he'd had a couple of drinks and then slept most of the way. But he couldn't ignore the feeling of discontent that washed over him every time he came back home now. Somehow life had become meaningless again.

~~~

Just fifteen years earlier, he had been so sure he was making a difference. He had just completed his MBA, landed his first real job, was making good money, and had Michelle, the love of his life. They had just gotten married, she was pregnant, and they were moving into their first "grown-up" house. Life was good, and Ben was hopeful. Better yet, he had evidence: life *was* good.

Many years later, his outlook on life had changed. The job was hard and Ben worked a lot of extra hours. In the beginning he hadn't minded. He wanted to prove himself, and the salary was good. But after a while he realized that something was missing.
~~~

He wanted to make a difference while he was on the planet, but somehow everything seemed to revolve around money. Money, power, and politics.

Michelle sensed that he was struggling. She was working part time as a substitute teacher and taking care of Emily, their daughter. Meanwhile, Ben knew he wasn't spending enough time with either of them. He hardly realized that Emily was growing up and that he had estranged himself from his family. He got used to zoning out in front of the TV. He gained weight.

Somewhere along the way, Michelle addressed the imbalance in their lives. For some time Ben worked fewer hours, went to the gym, and contributed more at home. Family life was feeling better. And then the recession hit and Ben was laid off.

For a while they lived off his unemployment check and their savings. Ben tried hard to find a new job—but he wasn't the only one. For each job opening he found himself competing with a hundred, even two hundred other job seekers, and employers could pick and choose. After a while, he simply gave up. He stopped working out, regained the pounds, and lost himself in his newest vice: playing video games.

Then Michelle, who was still working as a substitute teacher, was offered a full-time position. From then on Ben took over caring for Emily, but there wasn't much to do; she was a teenager now and was hardly ever home in the afternoons. Ben had no idea how she was spending her time or with whom. She talked about girlfriends and homework when she came home but she also smelled of cigarettes. Ben could feel her slipping away.

One day Michelle came home and told Ben she was leaving him. She had received a job offer for a good position near her hometown where her parents still lived. Emily would go with her. A change of scenery would be good for both of them, she said.

Ben nodded and turned back to his video game.

He barely noticed when Michelle and Emily moved out. They didn't pack much and didn't take any furniture, and for weeks Ben couldn't shake the notion that they would both come through the door any minute now. He played video games for weeks at a time—those were enemies he could defeat. He only needed the right set of weapons, some armor, and a good strategy. He was so skilled by this time that he could move through time and space almost effortlessly. He rarely lost a battle.

As the days passed, nothing seemed to reach him in his screen-blind stupor. Sometimes he didn't even know if it was day or night. His unemployment compensation always arrived on time, and he had given up hope of finding a new job a long time ago. He just sat there, waiting for Michelle and Emily to come home, his phone mostly turned to silent. He didn't respond to emails or texts.

One day he fell asleep and dreamed that he was standing in the middle of a street. The asphalt was wet, as if it had just rained. Ben looked up at the sky and noticed a few bulky cumulus clouds. He saw no cars on the street, in fact not a single person anywhere. He wondered where he was; the area was entirely unfamiliar to him.

Then he noticed a man standing in the street, about ten yards away. Where had he come from so suddenly? Ben looked more closely. That wasn't a man—it was an angel! He had the face and body of a man, but the two large white wings that hung down from his sides were clearly angelic. He casually looked over at Ben and smiled. His face was masculine, with even features. He was of average height and build. His hair was a little different from how most men would wear it these days, but well-kempt. He wore white clothes or some kind of a robe: *Like a Roman,* Ben thought. Yes, in fact, he did look a lot like a Roman marble statue, his skin smooth and its tone pale.

He responded to the being's friendly face with a smile. He knew he was dreaming, but he was still intrigued by the angel.

"Hi," he offered. The angel didn't reply but slightly nodded a greeting. Still smiling. *Fascinating,* Ben thought.

The mysterious figure exuded a gentle calmness: "peace" was the word that came to Ben's mind. He felt relaxed in his presence and was surprised to experience a wave of affection for this "man-angel." He started walking slowly toward him. He wanted to ask him something, but he didn't know what exactly. He had to admit that the whole situation was completely absurd.

The closer he came to the angel, the more at peace Ben felt. He wanted to shake his hand, touch him. Suddenly he heard a voice say, "Daniel."

He stopped in his tracks and peered at the angel. Was it the angel's voice he'd heard? Was he telling Ben his name? But how could that be? Ben was pretty sure his lips hadn't moved. He was still simply smiling and looking directly into Ben's eyes. Then he turned his head slightly, seeming to be listening for something. Ben followed the angel's gaze, but saw nothing, and when he looked back, the angel was gone.

"What the—" The words were stuck in Ben's throat. He was alone again, on an unknown street wet from the recent rain, in a strange city. He looked up at the sky and searched the clouds, looking for the angel—Daniel, that had to be his name—but he had vanished.

Ben woke up from his dream feeling uncomfortable. His face was wet: he had been crying. He felt a pain in his heart that he couldn't rationally explain—except that he missed Daniel! And the feeling of being at peace. There had been such familiarity and a sense of comfort emanating from his being, and he wanted it back. Ben lay awake for a while before falling back asleep.

The next morning Ben remembered his dream, and he addressed the angel.

"Listen, Daniel, if you're up there, I could really use some help."

He shuffled to the bathroom and looked in the mirror. His face looked bloated and pale, with dark circles under puffy eyes. He hadn't shaved in many days, and his hair urgently needed a good cut.

"You're right, my friend. This is it," he said, partly to himself, partly to his dream angel.

He shaved and took a long shower. He found clean clothes. For the next two hours he cleaned up the house. He washed multiple loads of laundry, collected many bags of trash, and took the bags to the dumpsters in the alley behind the house. Then he cleaned out the fridge and fixed himself some breakfast, having found some edible leftovers in the freezer compartment. He sat down and started rethinking his life. He had hit rock bottom; there wasn't any further to go. He didn't have a job and his family had left him. He felt useless, unwanted.

"Do it, Ben. You can do it," he heard a gentle voice say. He turned around, searching, even though he knew nobody was there. It was probably just his own voice in his head, he decided. After months of playing video games and eating an unhealthy diet, he wouldn't put that past himself.

Ben opened his laptop and started looking for jobs. After three hours he had sent fifteen applications. When he'd last looked for work, he had only considered jobs in his own city, but with Michelle and Emily gone there was no reason not to extend the radius of his search.

He applied for any position he was more or less qualified for. Most of these jobs and their descriptions didn't necessarily conjure up good memories—they were all outside sales jobs like the last one he'd had—but he had to start somewhere. He could still change direction later on, or even change careers entirely.

He found himself humming a melody; he hadn't felt this good in a long time. He was finally breaking through this rut! But when he went outside to pick up the mail he found a large envelope from Michelle. Divorce papers.

A note clipped to the pile of paper read, "We won't be back for a while. I think we should sell the house. Let's talk later."

Ben went back into the house, carelessly threw the documents on the dining table, and started a new video game. It usually numbed any pain he was feeling, but this time it wasn't working. And just an hour ago he had felt so good—back in action and ready to take on the world again.

"Daniel," he called to his angel, "I don't want to lose them!" His throat tightened and tears burned behind his eyes. Was this the end? Would Michelle really divorce him? What about Emily—would he still be able to see her?

He felt a presence, a soothing, serene energy right beside him on his couch. There was clearly nobody there but he heard that gentle voice again, saying, "Don't give up."

"Damn right, I won't!" he responded to the voice. He swallowed hard, turned off the video game, and went back to his computer. He applied for three more jobs.

Just two days later Ben was invited to a job interview at a pharmaceutical company a couple of hundred miles away. They were looking for someone to sell their new product to doctors and hospitals. They also wanted someone to train other salespeople and share management of the sales department. Ben had worked in this field before, and the salary sounded great. Within two weeks Ben had the house fixed up and listed it for sale. He found that he couldn't part with most of the furniture, which reminded him of happier times, so he put everything in storage. A week later he had moved to his new city where he rented a small apartment. He would look for something bigger later on.

Ben immersed himself fully in his new job, made progress quickly, and was soon one of the leading salespeople. He was traveling quite a bit, visiting various cities and their hospitals, and was building a steady client base. He felt successful.

One day he read some medical reviews about a product he was selling. Not being a scientist himself, he usually went by what his company and its own researchers told him, and according to them this drug was *the* new remedy for depression that America had been waiting for. Yet the independent reviews concluded that not only did the product fail to deliver on the company's ambitious promises, but it had already been associated with some dangerous side effects.

~~~

This was the situation weighing on Ben's mind as he let his foot off the gas pedal and glided down the on-ramp. He did his best to sweep his concerns aside. At least the FDA had approved distribution of the drug, Ben figured, though he knew they hadn't performed their own independent clinical studies. He would present these reviews during the next management meeting and find out what his superiors thought of them. He could only hope that investors wouldn't get spooked and sell the company's stock. He had invested in the company himself and had been following the stock price's steady upward progress with satisfaction. He didn't want to see that turn around. But the company had already dodged a few bullets and the product was still on the market and selling well, so maybe it would all work out for the best.

Ben parked his company car—a luxury model—near his apartment and checked his phone. Michelle had sent him a text message. She had congratulated him on his last big sale. That was nice of her—but she was also asking him when he would sign the divorce papers. He decided not to text her back.

He unloaded the car and rolled his luggage through the simple apartment complex he was calling home for now. He would look for something bigger soon, but for now he was quite
~~~

happy where he was. It was central, had a nice gym, and was in walking distance of a park where he sometimes went for a run.

Tomorrow was Saturday. He would sleep in, hit the gym, and then work from home for a little while.

2. To Find a Friend (The First Lesson)

Ben left the gym at around noon, went to his apartment, and took a nice long shower. He was feeling adventurous and wanted to try a new restaurant for lunch, a burger place a few miles away. Jackie, one of his neighbors, had told him about it. He hesitated for a moment and thought about calling Jackie and asking her to join him. She was attractive and nice, and as far as he knew she was single, but he didn't feel like it. In his heart he was still committed to Michelle.

When he left the apartment the roads were wet from a recent rain shower, but the sun was emerging from behind thick cumulus clouds. Ben relied on his GPS—and got completely lost. He entered an area that seemed vaguely familiar. He saw no cars on the street, in fact not a single person anywhere. Ben drove around slowly, looking for a street sign to help him orient himself, and suddenly hit the brakes.

"Darn it," escaped him. And that was all. In the middle of the street there stood a man.

Ben drove to the curb, stopped the engine, and got out. He approached the stranger carefully. He was wearing jeans, sneakers, and a gray sweater that read CHICAGO. He was of average height and build, his hair a little long but well-kempt. He was just ... standing there, looking down at the asphalt, seeming to be lost.

"Hey there, are you okay?" Ben asked warily. "Are you lost?" How strange to be standing still in the middle of the road. Ben couldn't help but feel a little annoyed.

The man lifted his gaze and looked into Ben's eyes. "Lost. Yes," he said softly, his tone warm. "Do you know where we are?"

We? Ben thought. "No, but I can give you a ride if you want." He hadn't intended to say that; it seemed to have come out on its own. There was something oddly familiar about the guy but he couldn't put his finger on it. He reminded Ben of something, or of someone he knew, a friend maybe?

Ben motioned the man to come along—he didn't want to just leave him there. He didn't seem to pose a threat, and he was too clean to be a bum.

He walked back to his car as the man followed. He was feeling oddly lightheaded. This situation seemed like an extraordinary case of déjà vu.

"What's your name?" he asked the stranger.

The man seemed surprised by the question. "I'm Daniel."

Ben stopped and swiveled in place.

"Really? Daniel?" he said, his voice rising in pitch.

"Yes, that's my name. I was sent here," he volunteered. "I don't know why. Something went wrong and I'm being punished. That's all I know."

"Sent here from where?" Ben lowered his voice.

Daniel gave him another surprised look.

"I don't remember." He shrugged. "I think from up there." He pointed at the sky. "But I don't remember a thing."

Now Ben was utterly confused. Was that *his* Daniel? His angel? Did he fall from the sky? Had he committed a sin and been sent down to Earth to be punished, as he said? Had he lost his wings? He almost looked like Daniel, but he lacked the angel's radiance—he looked more human, and there was no hint of a marble statue about him. *He still looks pretty blissed out, though,* Ben thought.

As they drove toward what Ben hoped would be a more populated area of the town, he couldn't help looking curiously at Daniel out of the corner of his eye from time to time. He finally recognized a few of the streets they were passing by.

"Where do you want me to take you?" he asked his passenger.

"I have no idea. I don't know where to go." He seemed calm and unperturbed in spite of this situation. Faithful, trusting that things would work out.

"Listen, don't think this is weird—" Ben started.

"What's 'weird'? What do you mean by 'weird'?" Daniel asked, seeming puzzled.

"I mean - you know … strange," Ben explained. He couldn't believe this. The guy was acting like he had never set foot on the planet before.

"I have a guest room," Ben started again. "You can stay for a couple of days if you like."

"Thank you," Daniel accepted. He seemed confused but not particularly concerned with where he'd be sleeping tonight.

"Or—do you want me to take you to the hospital? Maybe you hit your head on your way down here?" Ben almost laughed at this but caught himself.

And Daniel didn't seem to think it was funny.

"No, I didn't hit my head. I just came down, that's all. They said I need to make up for it and then I'll be allowed back. That's what I remember."

"Did they say how they want you to make up for … it?" Ben asked, simply curious now. This was getting better and better.

"Ten lessons. I need to review ten lessons." He paused. "I need to find a friend. Lesson number one. I think I found one?" He looked at Ben questioningly.

Ben nodded. "Sure. I'll be your friend. What's lesson number two?"

"I don't know yet. They will tell me later."

"Who are 'they'? Other angels?" Ben felt ridiculous the second the question slipped out. Daniel probably thought his new friend was very, well, weird.

But Daniel simply said, "Yes."

A chill raised goose bumps on Ben's arms and legs. Could it be true? Was this really Daniel, *his* Daniel, the angel from his dream? The invisible presence who had given him such encouragement and support when he was at rock bottom?

"Why did they want you to look for a friend?" Ben asked. "I mean, obviously you need a ride and all that, but wouldn't it be easier for you to travel alone down here? Meet all sorts of other people too? Carry less baggage?"

Daniel took a moment to respond. When he did his words were slow, deliberate.

"If you find one true friend, you are ready for a relationship with God. God is in all of us."

"I guess that makes sense," Ben mumbled. He found he was moved by what Daniel had just said—it seemed profound. He had never thought about friendship that way. He had a few people in his life he considered good friends, but his best friend had always been Michelle. Together they could have made it through anything … well, almost anything, apparently. But he never thought their friendship had made him ready for a relationship with God. And what did that even mean?

He hadn't really known God in his life. Sure, there was the old white man with the beard; that was the God he pictured. But a "relationship" with God? As in give and take, communication both ways? That just seemed absurd. He thought about all the people who prayed to a God who never physically showed himself. Ben felt sorry for the poor losers who placed their hopes in an invisible entity instead of getting up off the couch and doing something to change their circumstances. Like he had!

Well, he thought as he scratched his chin, *I only got off the couch after that dream I had, the one about the angel.* The angel Daniel, who Ben had to admit looked a lot like his strange new friend.

If God was in all of us, like Daniel had just said, was God also in him, in Ben?

He frowned. "Okay, I'm not sure I agree with that. God is in all of us?"

Daniel smiled. "Why, yes. You were created in God's image. Have you not heard that before? I think your human scriptures talk about that."

"The Bible?" Ben asked. "Well, I'm not really a Bible-reading kind of guy." He was starting to feel uncomfortable. He had been raised Christian but never had much of a connection to organized religion.

"It doesn't matter," Daniel said. "Many different scriptures say the same thing. When we find another person to love—for a relationship, marriage, or a good friendship—we are really just trying to find a connection to God. The purpose of marriage, according to many teachings, is not just to start a family and have children but also to help one another get ready for a real relationship with God." He paused.

Ben was intrigued. "That sounds interesting. Please elaborate."

"You humans," Daniel started. "You love each other so much! You don't even know if you've found a matching partner in a new love interest and you're already head over heels in love. How do you explain that?"

"Hmm." Ben thought about that. Good question. "Hormones?" he offered.

"That's certainly part of it," Daniel said. "But think about it. What do you experience when you fall in love? Besides all the physical aspects of it, including longing, lust, and hormones. What goes through your heart and mind?"

"With Michelle I thought 'I hope this is the *one*.'"

"What else?" Daniel prodded.

"Maybe something like 'I hope she won't think she's totally out of my league. I hope she can accept me for who I am—and who I'm not.'"

"So there was hope, right? You were hoping for those things?"

"Yes, sure. I couldn't be sure she wouldn't reject me, but I loved her so much that I was very much hoping she would accept me."

"Love gives people hope. Humans fall in love because they want to have hope. As long as there is hope, there is love. You still hope Michelle will come back to you, don't you."

Ben frowned. *How did Daniel know that?*

"Yes, I do."

"And you still love her?"

"Yes. I think I might never stop loving her. Whether she comes back to me or not."

Daniel laughed. It was a good-natured laugh but his next words sent a shiver up Ben's spine.

"For humans, there is a very fine line between love and hate. Humans turn their backs on each other when they feel rejected or unloved. They give up hope. They stop loving the other person when they lose the hope that the other person loves them.

Yet as soon as there is hope again, they realize they still love that person."

"Okay ..." Ben agreed reluctantly. It made sense. "I get it. Love and hope are interconnected. Now, how can we prevent that cycle of love, hope, rejection, hopelessness ...?"

"You need to realize that you are really just trying to find divine love. It is possible to find divine love in human relationships, no doubt. But it takes something special. For instance, both humans involved need to understand that they came together for the purpose of finding God. That their union isn't about material values, or security, not even about perpetuating the human species and having children. They came together to help each other attain a relationship with God, a higher, divine love. That higher, divine love is more pure than the love they have for each other could ever be." He paused to look at Ben for a moment.

Ben was trying to remember what had brought him and Michelle together so many years ago. At that time he didn't think God, or divine love, played a part in it.

"Drops in the ocean," Daniel continued, "are only drops of water by themselves. They would shrivel up and evaporate if they were isolated. So they try to find a way back to the ocean where they came from. Humans are just like that. Aren't they constantly looking for love, for being loved, and for people they can give their own love to? Their parents, siblings, girlfriends, or boyfriends and then spouses, children, very good friends ... Being with another human, for example a spouse, on the same path is wonderful because of the companionship and support, and to make the journey a little easier. Eventually, both drops want to be reunited with the ocean. And that is what divine love is all about. It's not really about the other person, who is pretty much just a traveler on the same path. It is about finding God and helping another person along, selflessly, with as much love and compassion for the other person as you can possibly muster."

"So you're saying that when we are in love with another person, we really just want to be in love with God? And that the other person is just a helper along the way?" Ben was still trying to wrap his mind around this idea.

"The love you feel for another person is of course real. You appreciate her and want to look out for her and love her, for all her brilliance and her little quirks as well. But she is just another human, like yourself. You both want to connect to a higher love—that's where your longing really comes from. You yearn to reunite with the ocean. And God gave you a companion to make the journey easier and more fun."

"Does that only work with spouses?" Ben asked.

"No, it works with anyone you have a relationship with that is based on mutual trust, respect, affection, and loyalty. Like a good friend. That's why we say, 'If you find one true friend you are ready for a relationship with God.'"

"And God is in all of us," Ben reiterated.

Daniel nodded, smiling.

"So God is also in me?" Ben was still having a hard time believing that.

"Yes, my friend, God is also in you."

"But how? What does that even mean?" Ben drummed his fingers on the steering wheel. He was beginning to feel agitated.

"Your true nature—your soul—is divine, eternal. That is the part that will go back to God when your body expires. Some people call that place of God 'heaven,' others 'the Universe,' still others 'the ocean of light.'"

Ben took a deep breath, shrugged his shoulders, and relaxed back into his seat. He was aware that he had a soul, of course, but he had never thought about where it would go once his body "expired," as Daniel put it.

He cleared his throat and turned toward his new friend. "I have to tell you something."

Daniel looked at him quizzically.

"A little while ago, I had a dream. There was an angel, with wings, his name was Daniel, and he looked like a marble statue, so perfect, and … like marble."

"That was me. I remember you too. You were very sad at that time."

"This is all true then?" Ben blurted out. "Angels, really?"

"Why not?"

"But angels aren't real. Only crazy people and hippies believe in them. And very religious people, of course."

"Think about the stars. They're up there shining all the time, even in the brightest daylight when you can't see them at all. Do you believe in the stars?"

"Yes, but that's totally different," Ben protested. "We can measure the stars with equipment, we have scientists for that. We *know* the stars are always there."

"So because humans haven't managed to invent equipment to measure angels, you believe angels aren't real," Daniel asked with raised eyebrows. He appeared more human himself than he was probably aware of.

"I guess you've got a point," Ben said. Michelle believed in angels and so did Emily, but Emily had also believed in unicorns for years.

"Okay, so now what?" Ben asked, putting off further discussion of the issue to a later time.

"Just keep an open mind," Daniel suggested. "I can't explain everything to you yet. But you believed in me once, didn't you? Why not now? Meanwhile, Ben, I might need your help down here. I don't know your world very well."

"Now that's a fact," Ben agreed. He thought about how helplessly Daniel had stood there in the middle of the street. If a car had come at him, would he have even stepped aside? Ben wondered: Had their meeting been preplanned? Was he really "lost" when he encountered Daniel, or was he supposed to find Daniel there? As he had in his dream?

He shook his head and decided to focus on driving. Still, he couldn't help but feel a tinge of excitement. *This is going to be interesting,* he thought.

3. Purification (The Second Lesson)

When they reached Ben's apartment, Ben parked the car and helped Daniel, who was experiencing some problems with the door handle, get out of the car. They stepped through the front door and Ben tried to hide his embarrassment. Not only had he not stored away his travel luggage yet, but he had also left the apartment in a hurry. Not just this morning. Every morning. He was considering hiring a housekeeper but he hadn't decided to make that commitment yet.

Daniel let his eyes wander over the furniture and other items in the apartment. His gaze stopped at the overflowing trash can. He gave Ben a questioning look—more raised eyebrows—and Ben hurried to explain that he was just back from a work trip and hadn't had time to clean up the place yet.

"Purification, discipline," Daniel began. "The second lesson. True freedom is not possible without self-discipline."

He walked over to the trash can, took out the nearly bursting trash bag, and held it up with his arm extended. They could both hear the soft plonk plonk of something dripping from it. Daniel looked at Ben, his expression more one of scientific curiosity than disgust. When he looked that way he reminded Ben of Mr. Spock from *Star Trek*: stoic and curious.

Ben hurried over and took the trash bag from him, grabbed some old newspapers and magazines he had stacked near the door for recycling, and carried everything out to the dumpsters in the parking lot. When he returned Daniel had already begun to pile dirty dishes into the sink.

"Daniel, you're right. This is no way to welcome a guest. Please, have a beer and make yourself comfortable. I'll clean up the place." He took two bottles of beer from the fridge, opened them, and handed one to Daniel. Daniel sniffed at the bottle and politely set it on the coffee table without drinking. Ben got busy collecting magazines, newspapers, and work reports from the floors and furniture.

"So, your place is real clean then?" Ben asked, trying to make light conversation in the somewhat heavy silence.

"Where I come from we don't have bodies. So, obviously, we don't need furniture, fridges, sinks, glassware …" Daniel looked around at the other items in the room.

"Your English is really good! How come you speak like an American? And you know the words for things like—the sink. Have you seen a sink before?"

Daniel thought before he spoke. "I was put in this body to have a human experience. My human host was from around here. He could speak your language, and he had seen a sink before. I am hopeful that if I pass my ten lessons I will be allowed back into heaven. Then I will leave this human body and only my soul will pass on. I think you have an experience quite like it here on Earth."

Ben swallowed a swig of beer. "Dying. We call it dying." He stared at Daniel. "I don't really want to see you die. Dude, really."

"This body would already have died. This man's soul has already left this plane of existence. I was able to possess his body at the same time he was leaving it." He paused. "Besides, the process of dying, the actual shutting down of the human form and the soul passing on, it isn't what you humans think it is. The dying process itself may not always be pleasant, but the passing of the soul is cause for celebration."

"How so?" Ben was intrigued.

"Immediately after death we are greeted by loved ones who accompany us the rest of the way into the higher dimensions. Then our soul meets the guides who help us review our last life time. There is no judgment or punishment, only a review—we get to see the good things and the bad things we did and how those actions impacted others. We actually get to experience others' emotions, as well as our own. This is where the soul grows and learns from its last life's experiences. Then we are allowed to rest, and after that we can decide whether we want to come back into another body or not. There is nothing but love up there. Endless, unconditional love." Daniel smiled.

"Wait … so are you saying that you have done all that? You were human before and then you died and became an angel, and now you're back to—what, revisit some of the lessons? Like in traffic school? You don't have to do the whole thing again, right? Just the lessons that you obviously missed?"

"I don't know about traffic school. My soul has been in many human bodies over many thousands of years, and I didn't have to be born as a human infant again. I was what you call an angel, a guide. Only higher advanced souls can become ascended masters, and I was on my way to becoming one of those. But I did something that I wasn't allowed to do, and that's why I had to come back down here. Whether we come back or not is our choice. I think in my case I was sent back to revisit those lessons on some kind of fast track, and hopefully they will let me continue with my ascension afterward."

"What did you do?" Ben was fascinated. He was still considering the possibility that he had brought home an escaped patient from a mental facility—albeit a very intriguing one—and he would certainly lock his bedroom door tonight, with Daniel in the spare room. But everything he was saying sounded truly fascinating to him. Ascended masters, higher advanced souls …

"I don't remember very clearly." Daniel said. "I am still trying to put it together. I think I interfered with the law."

"You guys have laws up there, like we do?"

"Well, we have higher laws. No one gets sent to jail where I come from—that's not necessary. But we do have to adhere to certain agreements. If we lack that understanding, we are not considered evolved enough to be in that respective dimension and we will be downgraded to a lower one."

"But you got downgraded significantly." Ben mentioned.

"I think whatever I did to break the law was significant too. I am glad I can revisit the lessons down here—time works differently on Earth. If you don't have a direct experience in a physical body, you miss a great deal."

Now it was Ben's turn to raise his eyebrows. "Is that so."

"There are so many things I can't explain to you yet, dear friend. Let's just take the lessons one at a time. I'm sure it will make sense over time. I'm not even sure what it all means yet."

Ben couldn't remember anyone calling him "dear friend" before; this was new. He cleared his throat. "Okay, so let's get back to self-discipline, the second lesson. From the look of things, you could say I might not have that down yet." Ben had gone back to the trash can and was cleaning up after the dripping incident.

"Discipline and purity of thought and action, is one of the very basic lessons. All we have is our word. Have you noticed that when you consistently think a certain thing, it actually comes true?"

"Yes, like a self-fulfilling prophecy. I'll say 'I can't do this' and then it turns out I really can't."

"Exactly." Daniel nodded. "What else? Do you have any other examples?"

Ben thought for a moment. "Well, when I get up in the morning and I tell myself 'It's going to be a great day' it usually turns out that way. But if I get up on the wrong foot, as we say here on Earth, sometimes the whole day is just one miserable experience after another."

"That's right!" Daniel really seemed to be getting a kick out of this; he was grinning like a child at Christmas. "As you can see, your words, or, if you haven't actually verbalized them yet, your thoughts, create your day for you. That's why it is so important to only think and say positive and empowering, 'clean' thoughts and words. And to be disciplined about it. The same goes for your physical surroundings. You want your living space, your work space, and—where else do you spend time?" he asked Ben.

"In my car?" Ben suggested.

"Yes, even your car. You want those places to be clean and comfortable, inviting peaceful thinking and creativity. A smelly trash bag, clutter, and strange green organisms,"—he held up a glass with a questionably green, obviously rotten substance—"do not contribute to that. Unless you are not aware of your surroundings. *Are* you aware of your surroundings?" He gave Ben a scrutinizing look.

"Most of the time I am, I guess … I really don't like the clutter or the green mold in my drinking glasses. I only notice it on the weekends though when I have a little more time. But I guess you're right. It's also not very healthy for our bodies."

"This is a vibrational matter." Daniel explained. "Clutter on the outside means clutter on the inside. How can you think, meditate, and connect with God if you're sitting in a pile of old newspapers?"

"I agree and … and I'm not sure about meditating," Ben admitted. "I did it once a long time ago, but Michelle, my ex-wife, she's the one who's into that kind of stuff. Yoga too. I'm not really the kind of guy who sits down on a yoga mat and hums 'Ommm,' you know?" He flashed Daniel an apologetic smile.

"Michelle … isn't she's *still* your wife?"

"Well, technically, yes. I haven't signed the divorce papers yet. We've been separated for a while and she wants me to sign them. I don't know why I said 'ex.' I guess it feels like we already got divorced but we really aren't."

"Why don't you sign the divorce papers, Ben?" Daniel's voice was soft, compassionate. Ben suddenly felt a burning sensation behind his eyes and a lump in his throat. He never cried in front of others, yet he couldn't remember when he had last felt this safe or understood. Tears welled up and his voice cracked as he spoke. "I can't. I want her to come back to me. I don't understand why she left me. Yes, I admit it, I was never home. I was working a lot. But I was doing it for *us*."

Daniel spoke gently. "Sometimes people grow apart, friend. Sometimes there is nothing you can do. Sometimes people only get together for a certain amount of time to learn some lessons, and then they are meant to do something else."

"But she's my wife!" Ben cried out. He felt like something was breaking apart inside of him. "Not just some girlfriend who grew tired of me. 'For better or worse, til death do us part'—ever heard of that?"

"Why sure, human marriage." Daniel shrugged. "There are a number of suitable partners for each soul, in every human lifetime. And then there is the One. The one soul that you will recognize among thousands of other souls. The one you are meant to be with, one lifetime after another. Are you sure Michelle is that One?"

Ben hesitated, then said, "I thought she was. We met when we were very young. We fell head over heels in love. We got married young too and our daughter was born soon after. I can't imagine being with anyone else. She was my best friend and I miss her." Tears started rolling from his eyes.

Daniel led Ben to the couch and gestured for him to sit down.

"It is difficult for humans who are unaware of their eternal souls to lose a partner. If you could only see, Ben, that you were here many times before. That you were married, in love, and had children many times."

"What do you mean? Reincarnation?" Ben looked at Daniel in disbelief and sniffled.

"Yes, you can call it that. Many of your earthly cultures believe in it."

"Yes but not many of our scientists."

"Oh, your scientists again," Daniel smiled.

"Nothing wrong with a little bit of science. I like facts. Evidence, you know?"

"Yes Ben, 'seeing is believing.' And someday, your scientists will develop machines and equipment to back up everything I am telling you." His broad smile covered his whole face. "Until then, how about a little bit of faith?"

"Faith? Oh please. You're not going to give me a scripture rundown … or are you?"

"People who live by faith, no matter what culture bore them, tend to fare better in life than those without faith. They seem to have more—here it is again—discipline. Now remember, without self-discipline no true freedom is possible. The mind will always try to engage you in negative thinking. But if you believe in a higher power, someone or something bigger and wiser than yourself, you might be able to release your burdens and worries to that power and find peace and solace in it. That's what we call faith. And the best way to access this higher power and your faith is through meditation or prayer."

"And you have met that entity bigger and wiser than yourself?" Ben asked.

"Of course. Up where the souls reside, there is no competition. We don't think in terms of 'bigger' or 'better' or 'wiser.' There is only love, eternal, beautiful love, and we are all One. The entity I am talking about is just that. Beautiful, loving Oneness."

"And you refer to it as 'God'?"

"Human words cannot describe that which is everything."

Wise answer, Ben thought. His tears had stopped and he was feeling a little silly now but he also felt relieved. He hadn't cried in a long time.

"We will talk more about this." Daniel got up and went to the fridge. "Do you have any food?"

"Sure, um, we could order something. Or go somewhere."

"You don't prepare your own food?" There they were again, those raised eyebrows.

"I don't really know how to cook. In our family it was Michelle who liked to prepare food. I know a couple of guys who are really great chefs, but they do it for a living. In this culture, us regular guys, if we're single, we probably eat out."

"Discipline also pertains to what you put in your body."

"What, now you want me to learn how to cook?" Ben's bewildered look made Daniel smile.

"Wouldn't you prefer to eat only things that nurture your body and your mind? That help you develop your senses and make the right choices, that give you so much energy you get all your work done quickly *and* have time left to contribute to others?"

"Oh, wow. Never thought about it this way. So what constitutes such food? I guess not the pizza and beer I have left in the fridge ..."

"Food has the highest nutritional frequency the closer it is to the Earth and the less time it has spent traveling or in storage. All your vegetables and fruits, seeds, nuts—everything you can pluck and eat straight off the trees or fields—constitute that. They still contain their mother's energy and vibration."

"Their mother?"

"Mother Earth. You have the same mother. That's why your body reacts well to those foods. You are related in frequency. Your body doesn't react well to processed food items, the substances that supposedly taste good but are full of artificial things that human bodies don't recognize and don't need."

"So what do you suggest? Start my own garden?" Ben laughed a little bit at that thought. He would need rubber boots and a wide-brimmed hat, and of course overalls, to look like a real farmer.

"There are entire communities that have started gardens and maintain them together. That's how humans used to do it. They farmed in communities and shared the work—and the harvest. I believe they still farm for the public and sell their harvest at markets. And you can buy healthy food items in your stores too, can't you?"

"Yeah, I'm pretty sure my grocery store has an aisle for organic vegetables. And there is a new restaurant I've heard about that's organic and vegan. For the single men who haven't started their own vegetable garden yet." He grinned. "Really, dude, I'm not going to start my own garden but I will give the whole high-frequency nutritious food idea a try." He looked around. "And I will clean up this place, and my car as well."

"And what about your thoughts?" Daniel asked.

"And I will make an honest effort to think only positive thoughts from now on. If I catch myself thinking negative thoughts, I will put on the brakes and think positive again."

"That's very good," Daniel said, seeming contented. "This concludes our second lesson."

"By the way, how do we know that you've learned the lessons? Is there a test?"

"My guides will decide whether I have learned the lesson or need to spend a little more time on it. You are part of my progress here because I am teaching you the lessons while I am reviewing them for myself. I believe that I will only be given a new lesson when we both pass the one before it. We will see if we get a new lesson for tomorrow." And he smiled.

4. Nonviolence in Word and Deed (The Third Lesson)

When Ben woke up it was already late morning. He had been up long into the night cleaning up, even scrubbing the floors, and making the apartment fresh and clean. He found Daniel sitting on the living room couch leafing through the Sunday paper.

"So much confusion," he was mumbling. "So much violence and greed. You humans really need to evolve to the next level of your consciousness."

Ben stared at him. "It's the Sunday paper," he said slowly.

Daniel looked up at him. "Why do you read this?"

"It's the Sunday paper!" Ben repeated, frowning. "That's what people do. They don't usually work on Sundays. They get up, make breakfast, read the Sunday paper."

"What purpose does it serve?" Daniel sounded concerned.

"It's information. It tells us what's going on in the world."

Daniel looked disgusted. He held the paper up pinched between two fingers, as if it were toxic. "*This* is information?"

Ben had no idea what he was getting at. He was still frowning.

Daniel continued. "These stories are about only a fragment of what's going on in the world. There is so much more happening than what fits on the pages of this so-called newspaper. Wouldn't you agree?"

"Sure," Ben said. "But it's impossible to report about absolutely *everything* that happens around the globe. Every child being born, every mayor elected, every war—"

"Every war, exactly." Daniel shook his head. "Reading this newspaper, you might get the impression that there are wars and tragedies everywhere. Recessions, political unrest, famines, violence, natural catastrophes all over the planet. But there is so much more to life on Earth than all the things that are mentioned here."

"Oh, I'm sure," Ben agreed. "But the newspaper sells better if it captivates people's attention. And most people thrive on drama and negative stories. It's exciting to them."

Daniel let out a deep sigh that seemed to come from the bottom of his soul. "We will have to work on that."

"About that ..." Ben sat down. "You were saying that the other angels might let you back into heaven when you learned your ten lessons."

"That's right."

"And you don't know what those lessons are until they tell you?"

"I knew that the first lesson was to find you, a friend. Someone who will be company on this journey. The second lesson was purification—both internal and external." He looked around the spotless apartment. "I think we passed that lesson with flying colors. Especially the external part of it. Good work, my friend." He seemed very pleased. "You are taking the lesson about purification to heart."

Ben was pleased too. He felt lighter and the world looked brighter. "I feel so much better now. I really didn't like the dirt. And I have only been thinking positive thoughts so far today," he added. "I might just cancel my subscription to the paper that you so criticized just now. And maybe I'll get rid of my TV. You can hardly find any good shows on it anyway, and the news seems skewed. And the commercials drive me crazy!"

Daniel laughed inwardly. He was proud of his student.

"So, what's the next lesson? Did you hear from your guides?

"I did. I dreamed the next lesson, and I am glad you're asking."

"All right, buddy, this whole thing had better not take too long. I mean, I am happy that my apartment is clean, but I have a busy work week next week and we might have to wrap this up pretty soon."

"Right. I actually wanted to talk to you about your 'busy work week.'"

Ben had a feeling he knew what was coming. He had become less and less satisfied with his job. Initially, he had liked the challenge, the level of responsibility, and his ability to act as a leader and propel the company forward. But he had recently read an article in the *New York Times* about their flagship product. Concerns were being raised about the very medication they were pushing so hard on the doctors and hospitals, making sweeping claims about its safety and effectiveness. Of course his company had already factored in the possible lawsuits that would derive from the occasional devastating side effects; all pharmaceutical companies did that. Ben wasn't really concerned but he had a nagging feeling and wondered whether what he was doing was appropriate. What if he wasn't making the difference he wanted to make? What if he was contributing to the greed and evildoings of a bunch of businessmen and stockholders who really didn't care about the people who were taking their drugs? What if there was another way to cure depression and anxiety? What if he was unknowingly promoting a big fat lie to make a few people rich? He was getting a nice paycheck himself as a leading sales rep, but was it all ethical?

He looked up and met Daniel's eyes. His new friend had been watching him as he tried to think through his situation.

"That bad, huh?"

"Well, I'm just not sure if what I'm doing is right. I wanted to help people. I really thought we had come out with an amazing product and we were helping a lot of patients who were suffering from depression and anxiety. You know ... I'm one of the good guys. I just want to make a difference somewhere."

"I know you are one of the good guys, Ben."

"Really?" Ben studied Daniel's face. He suddenly felt a real connection with this man … angel … fallen angel. Yes, he guessed that was what Daniel must be. A fallen angel.

"I think you should take a few days off. You have worked hard. You need a break, and you need to reevaluate your life." Daniel said it matter-of-factly, as if saying, "You need to go to the dentist." As if taking time off was an act of maintenance.

Ben smiled. He felt like he really wanted to take a few days off. He didn't know about reevaluating his life or not, but a couple of days away from the company might be just what he needed.

"The third lesson is about kindness," Daniel continued.

Ben looked surprised.

"Kindness and nonviolence," Daniel went on, "in word and deed. It means to take care of the body and the mind, to be healthy on all levels. To be kind to oneself and others."

"Okay ..." Ben weighed that new information. "How do I do that?"

"Well, obviously you avoid being violent toward yourself and others. You also speak kindly, think positive thoughts, and overcome any negative habits that would harm yourself or others."

Ben tried to think. "Like what? I'm already getting rid of the paper and TV."

"There's more," Daniel continued. "Negative thought patterns, self-criticism, addictions, indulgences—"

"Wait a minute. I need some of my addictions. I like to drink beer and coffee. I like video games. Although I haven't played since I got the new job because every time I played I really got sucked in and then I was playing for hours, especially at night. I had a hard time getting up and functioning at work the next day. So I scrapped that altogether and I don't even miss it."

"There you go," Daniel smiled. "The key is to replace a negative habit with a positive one. One that moves you forward in your development, helps you grow and feel good about yourself."

"Like exercising. I've lost weight since I started running again and I love how it makes me feel. Video games just zapped my energy. They were just a way to 'escape reality,' as they always say."

"It's important to honor yourself and that includes your body. Food is another thing humans use to escape reality, especially the stuff you call 'comfort food.'" Daniel shook his head. "It is better to meditate and practice self-study, and find comfort there if one feels uncomfortable with life and its emotions."

"Michelle took me to a meditation session once, a few years back. It was really interesting. I remember that I felt calm afterward and work was much easier for the rest of the day. I only went that one time though."

"I think we should meditate right now. Do you want to?" Daniel asked. He had a hopeful, almost childlike expression on his face and Ben didn't want to disappoint him.

"Sure, why not."

"How about right here, in your living room."

"Okay, but only for a few minutes, and then we'll get some breakfast. What do you think?"

"Sounds good."

They sat down together on the living room carpet.

"So what do we do?" Ben asked.

"First find a comfortable position where your spine is straight and your vertebrae stack on top of each other. No hunching over."

Daniel folded his legs and sat cross-legged. Ben followed his example.

"Next, close your eyes and just listen to your inhales and exhales."

Ben closed his eyes and listened to his breathing.

"Meditation is a great way to calm down the busy mind and to practice being present," Daniel explained. "Humans spend so much time thinking and worrying about the past and the future. They're not really present. But the present is the only time when we can truly create. Change, for example."

"I already feel calmer," Ben said with his eyes closed. "Just listening to my own breath makes me forget about everything else."

"That's good," Daniel smiled.

They were quiet for a few minutes, simply listening to their own calm breathing.

"When you feel your mind wandering," Daniel continued softly, "gently bring it back and just start listening to your inhales and exhales again."

Ben laughed quietly. His mind had indeed just wandered off toward breakfast. He hadn't even noticed. He focused on his breathing again.

After a while Ben felt extremely relaxed. Nothing seemed to matter. All he was present to was his breath and his breathing angel friend next to him. He felt a sense of oneness with Daniel, and a oneness with everything. *So that's what Daniel was talking about*, he thought. *Oneness with all that is.* He smiled.

For a moment he felt surrounded by other beings, not just Daniel. There seemed to be a warm, comforting energy coming down from the ceiling, embracing them both.

Yup, guys, we're friends, Ben thought. *We passed the first lesson a while ago, remember?* He smiled again. And then he thought, *I am talking to invisible beings!*

He focused again on his breathing and on feeling the energy that seemed to come from a higher dimension. He felt like he was connecting to it. It seemed like there was a whole other world up there, a world of wisdom and clarity that was missing down here most of the time. He decided to explore that connection a little more on his own later. Now that he knew how to meditate—all he had to do was close his eyes and listen to his own deep breathing—he could always come back here.

After a while Daniel stirred. He let out a deep exhale and spoke softly.

"Many of your teachers on Earth talk about meditation as a tool to quiet the mind," he began. "But you can also use it as a tool to work through unpleasant emotions, like fear or sadness or anger. Humans typically don't want to feel those unpleasant emotions so they repress them."

"Humans tend to repress their suffering in general," Ben muttered.

"That's right!" Daniel said. "And then what happens?"

"If I feel sad or angry, or if I just feel unsettled or grumpy, I do something to distract myself. Like how I used to play video games for hours at a time. These days I watch TV or tend to drink a little more than I want to. It seems to numb my thoughts and feelings. And then I go to bed. Sometimes I go to the gym to blow off some steam."

"There are many different ways to numb unpleasant thoughts and feelings. The main thing is that humans invite other energies in to suppress those negative ones. But over time it creates bad circulation. Like in your body, when your blood is not circulating well, it gives you a headache, right?"

"Right." Ben got the picture.

"The same is true with regard to your consciousness. If you practice suppressing your emotions, you create bad circulation in your mental formations, such as fear, anger, sadness, and suffering. Sometimes, because things are not circulating properly in the conscious mind, the symptoms of mental illness appear. Depression and stress."

"Is there a way to prevent that?" Ben asked.

"Yes. Opening your mental doors so the suffering can come out. Welcoming the pain and working through it to see its source. Not suppressing it and letting it manifest in the mind but taking care of it. Lovingly inviting it to speak to you and to tell you where it comes from."

"But what if it comes from a very deep, dark place, and once unleashed it will wreak havoc on your life?" Ben asked, worried.

"It can't," Daniel said calmly. "Once it comes out into the light it will dissipate, the way the memory of a nightmare disappears at first sunlight. It is vital to allow the pain to come out and speak to you. Once you practice directing your awareness to it, it will have no place to go. It will come out and disappear."

"Some people have very evil ghosts in their past," Ben challenged Daniel. "You don't think it would be terrifying to confront those?"

"Maybe for the first moment or so. It takes courage to confront your ghosts. But that moment doesn't last long. It is like the human fable of the mouse and the lion—ever heard of it?"

Ben tried to remember this story from his childhood. "Jog my memory, will you?"

"The big mighty lion lies in his cave, taking a nap. The little mouse is looking for some shade and enters the cave. Just at that moment the lion wakes up and stretches. He sees a huge shadow on the wall—the shadow of the little mouse in the entrance of the cave, cast by the sun. The lion, the king of all the animals, stares at the shadow in horror and fears for his life. He runs out of the cave, terrified. The mouse looks after him in amazement. The lion hadn't even noticed her when he ran past."

Daniel and Ben both laughed at that cute children's fable.

"This just goes to show that we often fear the shadow more than the actual experience," Daniel said. "If the lion had been able to see the mouse for what it was, a tiny mouse, he would have been able to conserve all his energy and not look like a fool."

Ben felt humbled. "I have run from a mouse's shadow on occasion, I am pretty sure of it. I just hope none of the other animals in the jungle witnessed it."

Daniel laughed heartily. "I am sure you are not the only one, dear friend. But this is why we need to look at our own 'mice.' Not just at the shadows they cast, which are so much more terrifying than the actual event from the past."

"I agree with you. I will start looking," Ben nodded. "That story was a great analogy."

"Looking at those events in your past and not getting distracted by their shadows goes right along with our third lesson,

Ben. Kindness and nonviolence in word and deed, for yourself and others." He smiled. "Let's take a break. You have been a very good student so far."

"Thanks, man. I have a very good teacher. Now let's go get some breakfast. I know a great little place down the street."

5. Truth in Word and Deed (The Fourth Lesson)

All we truly have is our word. Do you remember that earlier we said that when you consistently think about something, it actually comes true?" Daniel asked as he munched a piece of kale. They were eating breakfast at a vegan restaurant that Ben had picked.

"Yes, like a self-fulfilling prophecy," Ben responded. "That was lesson number two, cleanliness on the inside and out. Clean, positive thoughts versus 'I can't do this.' Because then I truly can't."

"Exactly," Daniel said, nodding. "As you can see, your word, or if you haven't actually verbalized it yet, your thoughts, create your day for you. They create everything around you. Without words—or language—you wouldn't be able to add meaning to a single thing. For example, a tree or a chair. How would you even feel about things if you didn't have a language to describe those things with?"

Ben thought about that for a moment. "If I didn't have the language to call a chair a chair, you mean?"

"Yes," Daniel answered. "Naming a thing gives it meaning. When in fact it has no meaning. Do you think a tree complains when it gets cut down?"

Ben frowned. "Well, it doesn't have words for it because it can't speak. But it sure 'feels' something, doesn't it? Wouldn't there be some kind of biochemical reaction inside the tree if it got cut down and cut off from the earth and its nutrients?"

"Very good!" Daniel was getting a kick out of their conversation, Ben could tell.

"Of course there are things going on inside that tree. Changes, death setting in. But does the tree complain about it? In other words, does it add meaning to what's happening?"

"Oh!" Ben felt a lightbulb go on in his head. "No, it doesn't! It feels that it got cut down, but it doesn't add meaning to that happening, like 'Oh boy, I had that coming. Life was just getting really good with all my tree friends around me, and now they had to come and end it for me. Of course, I never have any luck.'"

Daniel chuckled. "Exactly. For the tree, there are no emotions. It has no thoughts and no meaning around being cut down. Now, the person who cut down the tree may or may not feel sad about it. Maybe *they* add meaning to it. Like 'What a beautiful tree. I feel so sad that I had to cut it down.' Or the other extreme—'That tree will be great lumber and bring me a lot of money.'"

"I get it. People add meaning and emotions to the things that happen. Because they have language to express their thoughts and emotions with. For the tree, it's just physical - or biochemical. So ... what does that have to do with our next lesson?" Ben asked.

"I will tell you, my friend. The next lesson—lesson number four—is about truth. Truth in word and deed. Being aligned with who you really are as a soul and honoring yourself and your word. Meaning that you don't give your word and don't make agreements if you don't intend to keep them. You don't speak lightly, but instead with honor. You speak the truth and don't gossip. And you take ownership for speaking powerfully, not talking about irrelevant subjects that do not benefit your quest to become a better person."

"Well, that's a lot," Ben said. "It's powerful, but it makes me think about all the times I *didn't* speak powerfully, or when I gossiped or complained. I guess complaining falls under this too, right? Just checking."

"Yes, complaining is also a powerless way of speaking. And you can make a distinction right there," Daniel nodded. "There are gossip and complaining. And then there is a conversation with the intention of changing or transforming something. You're not gossiping or complaining if you have someone in front of you who is willing to listen to you with the same intention."

"The intention of changing or transforming something?" Ben asked.

"Right. Then your speaking is powerful. You're maybe bouncing it off your friend who is also seeking a solution. Or you are actively working through a problem. There's nothing wrong with that. As long as your intention is to truly create change in that situation or circumstance."

"And gossip is just that, gossip."

"Correct. Gossip is hugely disempowering. People who gossip aren't really interested in changing anything about that circumstance. Their ego feeds off the negative energy that gossip causes in themselves and others. It's a negative habit that leads nowhere."

Ben thought for a moment. "Some of the people I work with like to gossip. You're right. It seems exciting at first, but then it feels so negative and empty."

"It drains your energy, doesn't it?"

"Yes, exactly! So how do I avoid it? I don't just want to stay away from those people who like to gossip. I wouldn't even be able to—sometimes we spend hours together during meetings or conferences."

"The polite way to avoid gossip is to simply remove yourself from it. You don't have to leave the room for that. You just turn your attention and energy toward something more empowering. Over time, people who gossip will get the message and stop gossiping themselves."

"What if it's just one person who's trying to pull you into a negative conversation? How do you get out of that one? You can't just ignore them, can you?"

Daniel smiled. "You can say something like 'I prefer not to spend any energy on that topic. Let's talk about other things. Did you see the game last weekend?' Keep it light, and try to engage them in a more positive conversation instead."

"Okay, I will definitely try that." Ben was excited; he could really imagine that working.

"What was the other thing you said?" he asked. "Truth in word and deed and honoring your word as yourself? What does that mean?"

"It means that you speak the truth at all times and that you don't give your word lightly. You only make promises and agreements that you intend to keep. And once you make them, you do everything in your power to honor your word—as yourself. That means you don't find excuses or skip corners. You do the work as it was meant to be done and on time. With honor."

Ben sat quietly twiddling his fork with a look of intense concentration on his face. Daniel finished his plate and gave him some time.

"So …" Ben said after a while, obviously still pondering what they were discussing, "I'm a mess."

Daniel raised his eyebrows.

"I mean, that's huge. You know? I'm seriously thinking now how dishonorable I have been in my living and speaking. How I do cut corners—and lie about it. Especially at work, but everywhere! Not getting work done on time and then lying about it and finding excuses, sometimes even blaming other people for it! And even if I do a report on time, I usually don't do it with honor. I finish my reports in a hurry, right before or right after the deadline." He let out a wry laugh. "I can't believe I'm doing that."

"It's okay," Daniel said with compassion. "You are not alone. We call this 'the human condition.' All humans have it."

"You make it sound like a disease," Ben grumbled.

"It *is* a disease. And a contagious one at that. It makes you humans feel 'not at ease.'" He smiled his broad Daniel smile—which really annoyed Ben at this moment.

"We're all sick then? So what's the cure?" he said curtly.

"Awareness. Just being aware of how you're living your life. Paying attention to the things that come out of your mouth. And the feelings that come up when you make a promise you already know you won't be able to keep. How does it make you feel when you do that?"

"When I make a promise I won't be able to keep, and I already know that? It makes me feel like a liar!"

"Exactly. So this is our fourth lesson. Truth in word and deed. Honoring yourself as your word."

Ben had relaxed again. “Okay, now where do we start? This seems really huge.”

“Do you have any broken promises in your past? Any broken agreements?”

“How much time do you have? Should I get another coffee? Or a beer maybe?”

Daniel smiled. “Let’s go for a walk. We drove past a park on our way here. Why don’t we stop there?”

Ben paid the bill and they left the restaurant. The park was only a few minutes away. Ben parked the car and they set out walking along a row of old chestnut trees in full foliage. Daniel breathed deeply.

“This is one thing I really love about your planet,” he said happily. “The trees! So much oxygen, so much life force! Do you feel this?” He pointed to the leaves, clearly excited.

“Yes, it smells good.” Ben said. The air was damp after a short shower, and there was definitely some vibrancy around those old green trees. “Except, of course, the trees don’t call it that.” He grinned.

“Oh, are you referring to our earlier conversation?” Daniel laughed. “Very good! The trees don’t speak about life force or oxygen—that is correct. They don’t have any feelings about it, or assign any meaning to it. Only humans do that. It’s what makes you so complicated.”

"I agree. It seems like life would be a lot easier if we didn't add emotions or meanings to everything around us."

"Like you did earlier when we talked about truth in word and deed," Daniel pointed out. "What was the meaning you added about yourself? When you realized that you hadn't always spoken truthfully or powerfully?"

"That I'm a mess," Ben said ruefully. "I lie, I cut corners, and I bend the truth. I have some books at home from the library that I haven't returned for years now! There's a friend from college, we had an argument years ago, I think I even punched him. We haven't spoken since then. I had accused him of hitting on Michelle. I was so jealous and drunk and he was my good friend. But even if he did, it shouldn't have destroyed our friendship. Besides, she wound up marrying *me*."

"All of those are easy fixes," Daniel said. "All you have to do is clean up the messes you made. Call your friend from college and apologize. Return the books to the library and pay the fee. And tell your boss where you lied or cut corners."

Ben snorted. "He won't like that."

"Probably not. But if you start cleaning up your messes and take responsibility for your actions and their consequences, and show him that you have a different way of being now, he will most definitely like that."

Ben considered that for a moment.

Daniel continued. "Pretty much every human on the planet cuts corners, lies at least occasionally, and finds excuses. If you show up as someone who honors his word as himself, who speaks and acts truthfully, and who delivers his work on time and prepared with honor, that makes you a very special human being. I believe your boss will be delighted, maybe even inspired. Just try it out."

"Okay, angel man," Ben said between his teeth. "I will give it a try."

"Good job!" Daniel exclaimed and showed his big grin.

"There was something else you said. Being true to yourself? What was it?"

"Right, thanks for paying attention. You're such a good student! Truth in word and deed also means being aligned with who you really are." He looked at Ben as they continued to amble.

Ben looked puzzled. "Being aligned with who I truly am?"

"Who are you, Ben?" Daniel asked.

"That's a heck of a question. Well … I'm a Caucasian male, an American, I'm thirty-nine years old, I'm a father—"

"I know all that," Daniel interrupted. "We don't care about those things. Who *are* you?"

"What the hell are you talking about?" Ben was clearly confused.

"Look in your heart," Daniel suggested mildly.

"In my heart. Well, I'm caring—I think. I care about my daughter. And about my wife, even though she wants to divorce me."

Daniel nodded. "What else?"

Ben frowned. "I work hard. I try to help people. I have a few friends, they would probably tell you I'm a cool guy—"

"This isn't a job interview, Ben!" Daniel laughed. "Relax. Think. What do you feel in your heart?"

"Dude, I have no idea what you're getting at. Feel in my heart, for what? For you?"

"Well, maybe. Or pick someone else, like your daughter."

"My daughter." Ben's eyes filled with tears. "I absolutely adore my daughter. She's the best thing that's ever happened to me." He wiped his eyes on his sleeve.

"There it is," Daniel said.

"Did I answer your question? Did I pass?"

"You absolutely did, my friend. Although I'm not sure that you know who you are now, I know who you are."

"Who am I?" Ben asked, curious.

"Well, first of all, you are a soul. You came from the same place I came from, the place you will go back to when you leave your body. That makes you a divine being. Your soul is immortal, timeless, infinite."

"Okay ..." Ben said, "and you already told me that yesterday. It was hard to believe then too."

"Also, you are love," Daniel said matter-of-factly. "Your soul is made of the same material that all other souls are made of. The stuff that the Universe, God's Universe, is made of. Pure love."

Ben stopped walking and looked at his angel friend, his jaw wide open. "Do ... do you talk to all your friends like that?"

"Only my human friends. Because my angel friends already know," Daniel grinned.

"Oh, that's funny. So just checking, but if I am 'pure love'"—he couldn't help but grimace as he said the words—"then why do I feel so little love, and even outright anger, if someone cuts me off in traffic? Just as an example."

"Because you are also human. You are a divine being having a human experience."

"Do you have any evidence for that?" Ben asked dryly.

"For your divinity?"

"Yeah, because I have never considered myself that. I don't feel that part. I know I am human, but I don't feel any divinity in this body."

"You can't feel it with your human senses. You can experience it sometimes, in dreams or in a deep meditation. Have you never had a glimpse of God, or of your own higher self, your immortal soul?"

Suddenly Ben remembered their meditation. "When we meditated earlier I experienced something really cool. I felt like I was one with everything. I was really relaxed and peaceful, and then it felt like there were other beings, not just you and me. They seemed to be coming down from above. It was a warm, comforting energy and it embraced us both. That was weird. I forgot to tell you. What do you think of that?"

"That, my friend, was divinity. You were one with it, for a short moment during your meditation. That is just wonderful. Those were other souls visiting you. Maybe loved ones who already passed on, or just friendly souls. Or maybe your guides. Do you know now what I'm talking about? You are part of this energy. Do you understand who you are?"

"*Yes*," Ben replied emphatically. Suddenly it was clear to him and it gave him chills. He was not just this body. He was an immortal soul.

"That concludes our fourth lesson," Daniel said. He sounded proud. "Truth in word and deed, honoring your word as yourself, and being aligned with who you really are as a soul. You should talk to your boss so we can check this lesson off the list. Oh, look, there's an ice cream cart!"

Ben shook his head as they made their way toward the ice cream cart. "Is that in alignment with who you truly are?"

"Absolutely!" Daniel boasted. "I am here to have a human experience. I might be on a fast track, but I can still experience ice cream. Besides, it's been a while since we last ate."

"You're going to be one chubby angel when you get back to heaven, you know that." Ben laughed and took out his wallet to pay for Daniel's ice cream. He didn't really like ice cream but he chose one for himself as well. They walked over to a nearby bench, sat down, and silently enjoyed their treats.

Ben felt an immense sense of peace come over him. He was immortal! That meant that his daughter was also immortal. And his wife. And his parents, and everyone he ever cared about. *They will never die,* he thought. *We will always be together.*

6. Being Present (The Fifth Lesson)

"Okay, John, thank you. You too." Ben hung up the phone and turned around to face a smiling Daniel. "You were eavesdropping, weren't you?"

"Of course! I was too curious! How did it go with your boss and the cleaning up?" His grin was contagious.

Ben shook his head in disbelief. "You were right. He loved the fact that I was cleaning up with him. I told him that my reports are never complete when they are due—I almost always have to come back with more information—because I never start on time. I tend to blame other people for the information that's lacking, but the truth is that if I gave them more time they would be able to deliver what I need much sooner. I took responsibility for that and told him that I will start gathering the data sooner so my reports will be impeccable, complete, and on time from now on. No more lying, blaming others, and cutting corners."

"I bet he was impressed," Daniel nodded approvingly.

"He was! He even acknowledged me for the courage he said that must have taken. He said that if all his employees had the *cojones* to take responsibility for their actions like that, if everyone showed that kind of integrity, we would be a lot more successful at what we do."

"And how do you feel now?" Daniel asked.

"Relieved. Liberated."

"Complete?" Daniel offered.

"Yes, complete. Like now I have a clean slate ahead of me and I can create something new."

"And did you ask him for time off?"

"Yes, and he said it's okay. I have a lot of vacation hours and he said I should really take some. I don't have to be back until next Monday. So we have a whole week to review and learn your lessons and get you back to heaven!" he joked.

"Great, I'd like to get to work then," Daniel said. Ben could tell he was eager to move on. "But I haven't received the next lesson yet. That means I need to spend more time on the last one—but I thought we finished it. I'm not sure what's wrong." Now Daniel seemed troubled.

"Hey, I've never seen you like this!" Ben said. "Are you worried?"

"I'm not sure what's missing, that's all. I reviewed our last lesson, truth in word and deed, and you learned it too and applied it, and that should be it. We're done with that lesson. But I haven't heard from the Masters. That means that either we didn't fully learn the lesson or there is some kind of preparation step we need to take before we get to the next one. I would like to keep moving forward ..."

"Hmm, tough one," Ben mused. He wasn't sure how to help. "Can you think of something the Masters might say to you at a time like this? To help you solve this dilemma?"

"They would ask me to look at what's bothering me. To spend time in reflection and meditation. And through that to find an access to what's missing or incomplete, simply by looking more deeply."

"Well, should we do that? Can I help?" Ben suggested.

"I feel called to see some of your world while we do that. Do you mind if we travel a little? Go someplace where it's beautiful?"

"Sure, where would you like to go? Like I say, I have a whole week off now."

"Is there a place with a high vibrational energy? With plants and animals and flowing water?" Daniel inquired.

"There's a national park a few hours' drive from here. It has mountains, creeks, lots of nature. Have you ever camped before?"

"I don't recall. I might have in one of my other lifetimes as a human being," he said. "Should we camp there?"

"I think it would be a good idea. I have a bunch of gear, two sleeping bags—you can use Michelle's. I have extra clothes you can wear if it gets cold. The nights are still a little chilly. There are some nice campgrounds near the water, running streams, lots of deer and other animals. We might even see a bear," he grinned.

"Great. Let's do it!"

~~~

They arrived at the campsite just before the sun set golden over the mountains. They pitched their tent, rolled out their sleeping pads and sleep gear, and started a fire in the fire pit. Ben had brought a camping stove and heated some water for tea. He was getting used to Daniel's tea habit and he was surprised to find that he liked it too. He hadn't had a beer in a few days now and he didn't miss it at all.

They went to bed early and fell asleep with the calming sounds of the creek running peacefully past their tent site.

~~~

The next morning they got up early, had some tea and breakfast, and prepared small backpacks for a day hike up into the mountains. They would be back at the campsite before evening, so they took only enough food and water for the day.

They were silent for most of their hike, taking in the majesty and beauty of untouched nature. Occasionally when the trail took a switchback turn, they stopped to look over the scenic valley that unfolded below them. They marveled at the impressive palisade of mountains that formed on three sides around them.

Once while they were taking a little break, looking out over the valley and the creek below, Ben suddenly gripped Daniel's arm. When Daniel looked at him, he silently pointed to a line of trees a little off the trail. A large mountain lion was slowly walking along an invisible path. It didn't seem to have noticed the two humans less than fifty yards away, or maybe it didn't care. Both men instinctively held their breath and watched the powerful creature disappear back into the trees.

"Did you see that?" Ben exclaimed in a whisper. He couldn't believe his luck. It had been a long time since he had last seen a large animal in the wild, let alone a mountain lion!

"That was beautiful," Daniel sighed, clearly impressed. "I felt her energy from here. Did you feel her energy?"

"*Her* energy?" Ben frowned. "How do you know it was a female mountain lion?"

"Oh, she communicated," Daniel shrugged. "She saw us but wanted to be left alone. She would have kicked our butts, though, if we had approached her."

They both laughed. "No doubt," Ben said. "I had no intention of approaching her. So … you can talk to animals."

"It's all energy, my friend. Once you're tuned in, you can hear them thinking."

They stood, shouldered their packs again, and continued hiking until they reached a meadow on a plateau. The trail led farther up the mountain, but they decided to make the plateau their turnaround point. It was getting late in the afternoon and they still had to hike all the way down again. They didn't want to arrive at their camp after sundown.

"I am so glad we came here," Daniel said, a little out of breath. They sat down on a large boulder at the edge of the plateau, overlooking the valley and admiring the snow-topped mountains all around them. They let their legs dangle and spent a few moments in silence, enjoying the view.

"I haven't hiked in a while," Ben admitted. "Michelle was big on camping. She dragged me out almost every weekend when we started dating. After Emily was born we did less of it, but we did take a few trips with her in tow when she was a little older. She loves animals and didn't mind camping at all. It was all just one big adventure for her. Same for Michelle." He smiled sadly.

Daniel tilted his head and then looked at Ben for a long moment. "I just heard my Masters. They told me the next lesson."

"What, just now? What did they say?" Ben turned to face him fully.

"It's funny. I should have seen this coming." Daniel snickered a little bit. "It was right in front of me."

"What was?" Ben asked, confused.

"I was so excited about moving forward that I missed it. I guess I really just wanted to race through this, but there is a saying here on Earth—'Haste makes waste.' Or something to that effect."

Ben still looked perplexed.

"Coming here was exactly what we needed. We learned the first four lessons so fast that we barely had time to apply them to your life. You were such a quick study that I thought we'd be done in no time! But there is value in taking it slowly, letting information sink it and processing it more deeply, and practicing what we've learned."

"I agree," Ben nodded. "So what's the next lesson?"

Daniel laughed out loud. "Oh, my friend. You are so impatient! Just as I was."

"So, what? The next lesson is patience?" Ben frowned. "Is that it?"

Daniel looked at him, pleasantly surprised. "Patience is part of it. The next lesson is on being present."

"Being present?" Ben repeated.

"Being present wherever you are. Having a full experience. Being present in the moment, knowing there is nothing wrong in any given situation, even if it seems like there is."

Ben fell silent, letting the new lesson sink it.

Daniel continued. "Yesterday I thought there was something wrong because the Masters hadn't sent me the next lesson. But I was simply called to slow down and move deeper into my own experience of what I thought was happening or not happening. The stillness here, the sound of the creek at night, our hike up this mountain, encountering that calm, powerful mountain lion and fully being in the present moment with her, and letting go of the desire to rush our learning and experience with the ten lessons—all of that *was* our lesson."

"We learned the fifth lesson and didn't even know we were learning it," Ben observed.

Daniel smiled. "That's right. The Masters were guiding us without our even being aware of it."

"So why do we do that?" Ben gazed out over the valley. In the late afternoon light, all the colors seemed to intensify with each passing minute. "Why do we always want to rush things? Why do we have such a hard time just being somewhere, sitting down and taking in the view? I mean, besides the obvious that we are all very busy earning money so we can pay our bills and all that."

Daniel thought deeply before he spoke. His head was cocked to one side and he seemed to be listening to something. "The Masters are answering that question themselves. They are saying—"

"You're talking to the Masters right now?" Ben interrupted. Daniel seemingly hearing voices gave Ben an eerie feeling.

Daniel looked at him. "Yes. I do that when I want to clarify something or when the question is very important." He raised his eyebrows, apparently waiting for the green light so he could speak without interruption.

"Okay, sorry, that's great. Please continue." Still, Ben cringed a little. The Masters were obviously benevolent beings, and Daniel was very in tune with them, but if this connection between them was really possible—what else was out there? What else was hidden from his view but apparently in plain sight for Daniel? And why couldn't he see and hear those things? And for that matter, why couldn't he talk to the animals too?

"You asked me why humans have such a hard time being in the present moment," Daniel spoke.

Ben nodded.

"It's true that most humans spend most of their time *not* in the present moment. Most of the time they think about the past or the future. They relive past moments and conversations or worry about their problems and how those might affect their future. They go through life mostly unaware of their current surroundings. Would you agree with that?"

"Well, yes," Ben said. "I replay old conversations in my mind, over and over again. I analyze conversations I had at work, with clients, coworkers, my boss. I chewed over *every* conversation I could remember having with Michelle the entire year before she left me, trying to figure out what exactly led her to do that, and what I could have done differently. And I constantly imagine the future, a future with her and Emily in it, and a future without them. Sometimes when I'm driving thinking about that I don't even remember driving. All of a sudden I'm at my garage and I have no idea how I got there. I'm just glad that my driving skills are so automated that I don't have to be present to make it home in one piece."

"That's very typical for humans," Daniel said. "Your mind is mostly preoccupied with thoughts regarding your past and your future, and you do your tasks, like driving, on autopilot. It's very common. Now, the reason for this is an innate feeling that you are not enough. That you are not able to attract to you what you need in the moment. You all try to crack some kind of invisible code that would solve the problem instantly, or at least make it bearable. But there is no such code. You cannot solve the problem and make it go away in an instant. All there is to do is to just *be with* the problem, to allow it to work through you."

"And then what?" Ben asked. "What does that do for us?"

"Most of you humans have no clue that you are divine beings in a human body," Daniel continued. "You think your experience here on Earth is real, that this is it. You don't know where you came from or where you are going back to. You honestly believe that you are born as humans and that the light goes out when you die. That's why you are all so scared, trying to hold on to things and people, grasping for material goods and money like your life depended on it. But if you saw that this lifetime is only temporary, just a tiny sliver of time compared to the big picture—to many lifetimes before and after this one, and many more opportunities to learn your lessons and to 'get it right'—you would all relax and simply *be*. There really is nowhere to get to. All you have is *now*. You might as well make the best of the present moment. Of *any* present moment."

They were silent for a while. Ben needed time to process this.

"So in terms of my failing marriage," he finally began, "you're saying I shouldn't be thinking about it, not trying to fix it by attempting to crack the code of what's been wrong with it because there is no code, but instead should just be with it and let it work through me? I don't understand. What do you *mean*?" he asked desperately.

"Okay, Ben, this is where it gets deep. Are you ready?"

"Yeah, sure, man, bring it on. We're already here."

"You've been thinking and overanalyzing for quite some time now, haven't you?"

Ben nodded.

"And it hasn't gotten you anywhere, right?" Daniel didn't wait for an answer. "You humans have up to sixty-thousand recurring thoughts in your head every day. Most of these are negative, repetitive, and redundant."

"Holy hell!" Ben gasped.

"That's what humans do. You all do it. You're on autopilot most of the time and then you start thinking. But it's not creative, problem-solving thinking. It's a repetitive mulling over of the past and the projected problems of the future. You with me so far?"

"Yes," Ben was listening attentively.

"Most people can't *be* with a problem. Why? Because they don't want the emotions that come with that—with being present with a problem. They think that their emotions will overwhelm them, turn them into mush or make them angry to the point of destroying things."

"I've had those moments," Ben admitted.

"It's part of being human, and it's okay," Daniel reassured him. "But if you can *be* with a problem, just feel the emotions it brings with it and accept that it is really happening, it will eventually go away. The feelings will lessen, and out of your acceptance other possibilities will arise. But first you have to accept it—the way it is *and* the way it isn't. If only you could accept that the present moment, *any* present moment, is perfect the way it is, that *you* are perfect the way you are, your life would be so much easier."

"I am perfect the way I am, in any given moment ..." Ben mulled this over. Then he started laughing. "Okay, man. I appreciate the sentiment, but I really don't see that."

Daniel answered with his good-natured laugh. "I know. I see what you see, your human body and human faults and human emotions. But you need to start relating to yourself as a divine being, living in a human body for now for the sake of learning and creating experiences. The learning, you take with you, by the way."

"Oh, that's cool. So I don't have to start at square one again the next time I come down here?" Ben meant that to sound sarcastic, but he was coming to believe that what Daniel was saying was true. He could feel it in his heart, and it was beginning to affect him.

"If you were actually perfect the way you are, in any given moment, and the moment itself is perfect too, what would you do about the current situation with your marriage?" Daniel asked.

Ben took a deep breath and exhaled. "I would relax. For once. I have been stressing about this for such a long time. I would rest. I would trust that it's perfect the way it is right now. That maybe we both need this time-out, for whatever reason I don't see or understand yet. Just like I don't hear your Masters but you do. Maybe there *is* a realm where everything makes sense. The bigger picture, as you said."

"That's exactly right, my friend. There is a bigger picture and a realm where it all makes sense. If you ignore the gift of time and want to speed up the process and rush into things, you will never be ready. You need this time of separation to figure yourself out. And when you are ready, you can powerfully create whatever serves you—and her. For example, completion. You could let her go so that she is free to love someone else." He ignored Ben's frantic stare. "Or you could get in touch with her and give her what she needs. And create a future together with her and your daughter, one that works." He paused. Ben sat quietly, listening and processing.

"Ben, instead of scarcity and a code to crack and the urgency to fix things, there is abundance. For all of you. Everyone will be taken care of. But it happens in the present moment. Not in the past and not in the future. Do you understand?"

"Yes," Ben said. "I don't have control over the past because it already happened. And the future hasn't happened yet and my thoughts and worries might not even affect it—unless I create a problem *because* of my worries." He laughed dryly. "So all I have left is the present moment. I can control what's in my power right now, and I am wasting time and energy by focusing on what's not, like things from the past and the future. Right?"

"You got it. And if you start controlling what's in your power right now and enjoy the present moment, you can do things more deeply, enjoying the full experience, and not miss out on life itself." Daniel smiled. He looked happy.

"It seems like a great way to take better care of ourselves too," Ben said, feeling infected by Daniel's contagious happiness. "Taking life slower, resting more, sleeping more, eating healthier foods, really taking the time to nurture our bodies and our souls, to exercise and not just rush to the gym for twenty minutes and then back to work."

"And that same kind of care and respect you can extend to others as well," Daniel said. "You are unique and so are others. You could meet each other with openness and curiosity instead of with preconceived notions and judgments stemming from the past."

"If everyone did that," Ben said, "that would change everything about humanity. People would actually meet each other with openness, not prejudice. Can you imagine?" He shook his head. "In another century maybe."

They turned to look over the valley again. The sun was low; it had touched the entire mountain range with pink and orange light. They sat on their boulder for another few minutes in complete silence admiring the valley and the mountains. Finally, simultaneously letting out a contented sigh, they grabbed their gear and started the hike back to camp.

7. Freedom from Attachment (The Sixth Lesson)

The next morning they woke up early again. They took their time over tea and breakfast. Daniel knelt on the sandy beach of the creek, looking toward the snow-capped mountains that rose majestically on the other side of it. "Do you feel this?" he asked over his shoulder.

Ben was pouring himself more hot water for a second cup of tea.

"Feel what?" He put down the camp kettle and joined Daniel at the creek. He stood there for a moment, feeling into the early morning air as the sun peeked over the mountains and the birds sang ... and smiled.

"Yeah, man, I feel it."

"The present moment. And it's perfect." Daniel smiled too.

"I don't think it gets more special than this," Ben said. "Out here where there are no people, no people sounds, just nature, mountains, birds, the sun ... this *is* perfect." They enjoyed the moment a little longer until Daniel spoke again.

"Every moment is perfect, my friend. If not special like this one, peaceful and inspirational, then perfect for our growth and our learning."

"Okay, well, what's perfect about the moment when you stub your toe on your bedpost?" Ben asked, trying to be witty.

"It's great for learning," Daniel grinned. "Children do that all the time. They stub toes, they fall over, they get up again. Have you ever noticed how children just carry on? They don't add meaning to falling over—they just get up and move on. Accidents happen. Stubbing your toe happens. Moving on is the lesson." He scanned the creek and the mountains again.

Ben was silent, processing how they were reviewing the fifth lesson - even that seemed perfect!

~ ~ ~

"What's the next lesson?" Ben asked. They had been driving for a while. It was hot and dry; nothing seemed to live in this desert climate except for small brush and the occasional tumbleweed. Even though Ben was enjoying his time off work, he was ready to solve another challenge and learn more about Daniel's "enlightened" way of being.

"Freedom from attachment. Or put another way, generosity."

"Just downloaded that, huh?"

"Yup."

"Alrighty. Generosity it is." Ben turned into a semi-deserted gas station. "And always good to fill up when you're driving through a desert and see a gas station along the way." He got out and started to fill the tank. Daniel got out and stretched. "I'm telling you. These human bodies are just too tight."

"Shhhh," Ben warned, grinning. An elderly man sitting on a bench outside the store had caught that line. He stared at Daniel, seemingly incredulous, and then slowly shook his head.

"So tell me about generosity," Ben said. "What do we need to learn here?"

"Well, most of you don't. Learn, I mean. Most people just want to survive. They think that making money and acquiring earthly possessions mean something. In the big picture none of that matters."

"Then what does?" Ben finished the credit card transaction at the pump.

"What matters is to be happy at every moment. To be generous to your fellow beings. And to not be attached to material possessions, in fact to be free of attachments, material and non-material."

"Be poor? Give it all away, you mean?" Now it was Ben's turn to give Daniel an incredulous look.

"No. But think for a moment. When were you at your happiest? When did you feel the most connected to all, to yourself, your family, your surroundings, other people, the universe? Think."

Ben didn't have to think long; the image came to him almost instantly. "When Emily was born. That was the happiest moment of my life. Time stood still. I couldn't believe what was happening. She was so precious. So fragile, so ... beautiful, for lack of a better word."

"That's right, you don't even have the words for it, do you?" Daniel nodded. "You were in touch with true being. With divinity. With creation. Did you believe you could have created that by yourself? That your daughter was entirely a biological product of you and your wife and nothing else?"

"No, there was definitely something else there," Ben said pensively.

"Divine creation."

"Yeah, something like that."

"So if you had a choice, would you trade that moment—if you could—for all the money in the world?"

"Of course not!" Ben said, indignant.

"That's right. You wouldn't! And yet, most people seem to think that money, power, cars, even expensive furniture make a real difference in their lives."

"Well, things like that make life comfortable. And they give us a sense of security."

"Of course. And by all means, live comfortably and make sure you can pay your bills. You humans seem to have a lot of bills. But what more is there besides food, clothes, a place to sleep, and the occasional entertainment?"

Ben wasn't sure whether that was a rhetorical question. He tried to answer it in his head but he couldn't really come up with anything. Travel maybe. Yes, traveling was expensive. Did that fall under "occasional entertainment?" He wasn't sure.

Daniel laughed. "Ben, you look confused."

"Well, I know money isn't everything. But are you suggesting that we should all ditch our worldly responsibilities and simply focus on watching babies being born?"

"I am saying that you find happiness when you are in the presence of creation. Creation that is beyond your own. When you are present to the greatness that life is and you feel connected to its Source, that's when earthly possessions start to lose their meaning. When you are connected to Source, you feel safe. Even without a house in your name and a car in your garage. Or even a car, for that matter. You feel safe no matter where you are and no matter how little money you have. You are a true child of the Universe and you feel protected at all times."

"Even if I live on the street and eat scraps out of trash cans?" Ben looked doubtful. He believed Daniel, but he didn't think he wanted to try that out. Maybe he would skip this lesson and leave it up to Daniel to solve it for himself.

Daniel was quiet for a moment.

When he spoke again his voice was kind, compassionate. "Do you want to know what's wrong with your planet?" he asked.

"Please, do tell."

"The problem is that you are all so afraid. There is so much fear here so you cling to money. Because you think that money means security. You think money will keep you safe and warm and fed."

"It does, though—doesn't it?" Ben asked.

"The clinging to it gives you all anxiety."

"Then what would you do?"

Ben was stumped. He looked at his angel friend and noticed for the first time that a faint light seemed to surround him. It was barely visible but it made his face shine. *His eyes are lighter too*, Ben thought. He couldn't look away. He wasn't sure whether Daniel had always glowed like this. *I've never noticed this before*, he thought.

Daniel responded to Ben's question. "Clinging to money doesn't give you peace. Faith does. Faith in the network that surrounds you all, that intricate, intelligent, benevolent organism that some of you call God. They will provide. Everyone will be taken care of, and more. Just ask for it, believe in it, expect it to happen, and they will give you everything you need. That is how this really happens. Not through fear and clinging."

Ben thought it through. "Just ask?" he said doubtfully. "What if I want a million dollars? Can I have that?"

"Let me ask you something, my friend." Daniel looked straight at him. His face was still glowing slightly, a little less than a moment ago. "What do you think a million dollars, or ten million dollars—because the Universe doesn't even see a difference between small and large sums—would provide for you? What would you use it for?"

Ben didn't hesitate. "I would pay off my debt. Buy a house. Buy Michelle a house, send Emily to college, buy a nice car, nice clothes, eat really expensive food—"

"And then what? What would those things provide for you? The house, the clothes, the car."

"Security. I would feel like I had it made. I would be ahead of the competition and I would feel confident and strong."

Daniel smiled. "You sound a little bit like a caveman right now. Did you notice that? Who killed the bigger mammoth?"

"That's the world we live in." Ben was feeling defensive now. "It's about who's got the bigger car and the bigger house. It might be lame where you're from—well, you don't have cars and houses so the point is somewhat moot, isn't it."

"Ben, you have no idea who you are!" Daniel's voice was still warm, but now carried some urgency. "You are beings of light! You are made of love! You are connected to Source, to God. You *are* God! The same God energy that's in the Universe is in you! That's your soul and what you're really made of! You are so powerful you can attract anything into your lives, and you do! You attract everything you continuously think about, good and bad."

Ben was stunned into silence.

Daniel continued. "But you all suffer from a sense of lack, of not being enough, and a lack of faith that you can create or attract what you need at any given moment. Hence the grasping. The comparison to others who seem to have everything. The jealousy, the envy. Instead, if you could just see that there is abundance, that there is enough—and more—for *all* of you, you would simply have faith and create whatever you need. All the good things you want in your life!"

Ben found his voice again. "If there is abundance, why are people homeless? Why are some people so poor that they can't eat, except for the scraps they find in trash cans?"

"That's really their choice, my friend," Daniel said mildly. "Some of these people are very old souls who came here to learn a specific lesson. In the big picture and for their learning, their problems and their poverty make sense. We are not to judge them for choosing that."

"You make it sound like there's nothing wrong with it."

"There *is* nothing wrong with it. Nothing that goes on around here happens by accident."

They were quiet for the rest of the drive back to the apartment. Ben's mind was filled with everything they had talked about, and he was starting to see a bigger picture. He had spent his whole life chasing after accomplishments. The degree, the jobs, getting better and better positions, selling more, achieving more, the house, the cars … and where did it leave him? Michelle and Emily left and he got depressed and addicted to video games. He worked his way out of that and found a new job, but now it was the same thing all over again. He was trying to get ahead and felt like he was killing his soul at a company he didn't believe in anymore.

If there was a bigger picture, what was he really here to do? If he wasn't supposed to just attract money and earthly possessions, what *should* he focus his time and intention on?

~ ~ ~

They arrived home after nightfall—and saw that the front door was cracked open. The second thing they noticed was that someone had burgled Ben's apartment. His TV set and most of his other electronics were missing. Someone had rummaged through his closets and drawers.

Ben walked through his apartment in silence. Except for the electronics, nothing seemed to be missing. His laptop was the only thing he would have missed if it had been stolen—it held personal information and company files—but he had brought it with him on their camping trip.

"Are you all right, my friend?" Daniel asked.

"It seems like only the electronics are missing, TV, video-game stuff, nothing else." Ben was astonished to discover that he didn't feel much anger about having those possessions stolen.

"You don't seem too upset. I take it those things weren't expensive." Daniel probed.

"Oh, actually they were," Ben replied distractedly. "As you know, I like expensive things. But somehow I don't really care about those, and that surprises me. I used to get so angry if people tried to steal from me, or sometimes even if they just touched my stuff. But I guess you opened my mind on our trip. I don't feel attached to those things anymore. After all, they're merely earthly possessions." He sighed, and realized it was a sigh of relief.

"Right on," Daniel smiled. "Just imagine the world the people who took your things live in. Entirely driven by fear, lack, and scarcity. How much pain there is for them! Can you feel compassion for them?"

"Oh, absolutely!" Ben turned to Daniel. "I am certain that those guys are afraid right now of being caught. And I think, somehow, what they did must have left an impression on their souls. I wonder how they sleep at night. And I believe they needed my things more than I did. Honestly, I'm kind of glad I'm rid of that stuff! I hardly ever watch TV anymore, and I can watch movies on my computer anyway. And after spending those couple of days in nature and complete silence, away from all the sounds that humans make, I almost feel like I don't want to burden myself with any extra noise."

He paused for a moment and then smiled. "I didn't need this stuff, you're right. I have all I need, and more. So much more. And it almost feels good now that I 'gave' it all to them, albeit involuntarily—I do wish they had asked." He laughed. "At first I was shocked that they broke in. But I understand this now. How much I really have and how little I really need. And how little *they* think they have."

Daniel's eyes widened and he shook his head, momentarily struck mute.

"What?" asked Ben. "What is it?"

"Nothing … I just almost can't believe how quickly you learned our sixth lesson. Freedom from attachment and generosity—you completely nailed it!"

"That was our lesson? You're right! I almost forgot … oh, I get it. So your guides had those guys break into my place in order for me to learn the sixth lesson." He couldn't believe the synchronicity of events. "Would you please tell them not to do that again? I am happy to give my stuff away without having complete strangers, criminals no less, snoop through my apartment."

"But would you? I guess the guides thought this was the perfect situation. Not only did you apply nonattachment to things you once deemed expensive and valuable. You also found compassion in your heart, even for these lowly criminals who so obviously trespassed and snooped through your apartment."

"You're right," Ben concluded. This *was* the perfect situation. "I guess your teachings are really sticking with me."

He gave Daniel a long look. "You are making a whole other person out of me, aren't you?"

Daniel just smiled.

8. Compassion (The Seventh Lesson)

The next morning when Daniel woke up, he found Ben meditating in the living room. He must have gotten up early because in the hallway were boxes full of books and decorative items from the living room. Ben opened his eyes and greeted Daniel.

"Your tea is steeping in the kitchen," he said contentedly.

Daniel took a second look at his friend's smiling face and smiled as well. "You seem happy. Did you sleep well?"

"I got up very early and felt so good! I had a lot of energy and decided to get rid of some things from the living room. Now that my TV set is gone, I don't need those shelves anymore. I'm thinking I might create a more Zen-like environment here. In fact, I feel like I want to move again altogether. Maybe get a little house somewhere more in nature. What do you think?" He looked expectantly at Daniel.

"That sounds like a great idea."

"I just feel so liberated right now. I don't need any of this furniture, really. Maybe something for guests to sit on, and a bed, and something to put my clothes into. And yes, bookshelves because I do have a lot of books. But I have way too much stuff. In fact, I'm going to go through my storage unit and sell or give away—probably just give away—what's in there. There are people who might need some good-quality furniture. For me, I'm not interested in that stuff anymore."

Daniel's smile stretched from one ear to the other.

"What are you grinning about?" Ben asked, although he couldn't wipe the grin off his own face.

"I am so happy to see you like this. You look light, free. You're really taking on that sixth lesson of ours, about generosity and nonattachment!"

"I feel entirely unattached right now. To my stuff at least."

"Okay, good point!" Daniel said.

Ben looked at him with a question mark on his face.

Daniel continued. "To your stuff, you said. There are other things you humans tend to feel attached to. Thoughts, ideas, people …"

"Oh, I see where you're going with this," Ben said, understanding now. "Letting go of negative thoughts or ideas that are outdated or have no place in my life anymore—even people, I get it. I tend to let stuff go pretty quickly, I think. Except for my marriage and my family, of course. And I won't let them go—you can forget about that." Ben suddenly felt defensive.

"Don't worry," Daniel replied. "I am not suggesting that. We are talking about letting go of the things that don't nourish you, thoughts and people that bring your energy down or affect you in a negative way. Those, you can let go, but not the people you care about." He paused. "Was there anything else you felt you wanted to let go of?" Ben caught a glimmer of mischief in his eyes.

His internal alarm bells went off. "What are you getting at?" he asked warily. In his heart he knew all too well what he had wanted to let go of for a long time—but didn't yet have the courage to do. Better to play dumb for a while and avoid the problem altogether.

But Daniel wasn't fooled easily. He could see right past Ben's efforts to evade the conversation. "Your unfulfilling job?" he asked.

"I like my job!" Ben became visibly agitated. "I just don't like selling a product that has serious side effects and makes people addicted."

"You like your job?" Daniel, eyebrows raised. "Seriously?"

"Daniel, come on now. What else am I supposed to do? I went to school for this, worked my whole life in that field. I was so glad I finally got a job again. I need money!"

"Are you unattached?" Daniel asked cautiously.

"What? No! I am not unattached. I need a job, an income, financial security. I am attached to being able to pay my bills and have a place to live."

"I think we need to review our lesson," Daniel said matter-of-factly. There was no judgment in his voice. "Why don't we go for a walk in the park and talk about it," he suggested.

~~~

As soon as they reached the park with its green trees in full summer foliage, they both started to feel better. Ben relaxed visibly.

He took a few deep breaths, drinking in the sweet oxygen of the trees. "I thought I had the lesson about unattachment down. I was willing to give the contents of my whole storage unit away. But I guess it's not that easy."

"Don't be so hard on yourself," Daniel said warmly. "Giving your material possessions away—of which you have plenty—and letting go of people, ideas, and perceived securities are two different ball games."

Ben smiled. "How do you pick up on those terms? Ball game? Have you ever been to a ball game?"

Daniel frowned in deep thought. "I guess my human host has, in his lifetime. It seemed like an appropriate expression."
~~~

"The problem is," Ben continued, "that I really wouldn't know how to go about it. I talked to my boss about the allegations that our flagship product is more or less a placebo with heavy side effects. A whole generation of depressed people is just getting hooked on it, or at least that seems to be our company's goal judging by how hard we're pushing this product on doctors and hospitals. We give them free samples and of course we reward them financially when they prescribe it to their patients. But do the patients actually get help? I doubt it. I used to really believe in this product. I thought it was the answer to a lot of people's problems. But now I have doubts."

"So how did the conversation with your boss go?" Daniel asked.

"Oh, well, he subtly reminded me that there are plenty of other people who would gladly take my job. He did try to convince me, though, that we're doing the right thing. If the public wants a drug, they should have it. Those weren't his exact words but something like that. We're basically doing them a favor, in his mind."

"Getting them introduced to a drug they didn't know about before and then getting them— 'hooked' on it?" Daniel seemed seriously concerned now. "And it doesn't even work?"

"Well, the placebo effect of it works," Ben explained. "People think they're taking a powerful medication, and that makes it work for some of them. Some people just want to take a pill and be better. But in other cases it makes people worse. Much worse."

He found the truth of his own words crushing. Daniel was right; he couldn't stay in that job.

They were silent for a while as they strolled around the park. Daniel stopped a couple of times to smell some flowers or watch a couple of squirrels chasing each other. He seemed to be having a great time again out here.

He is fully present, Ben thought. *Here, right now, with no thoughts about the past or the future. Just happy and in the moment.*

Daniel returned his attention to Ben. "Well, Ben, now what?" he asked. "Look at it this way—if you were unattached, what would you do?"

Ben's response came almost immediately. "I have some savings. I would quit the job tomorrow. Live off my savings, downsize a little, not spend so much money on food at expensive restaurants, live a simpler lifestyle, and find a new job. And report our drug to the officials who could actually do something about it. Or to the media, or both. I don't know yet."

Daniel smiled. "How would that make you feel? If you quit tomorrow?"

"A lot more at peace. Liberated, like it's the right thing to do and I know it."

They fell silent again while Ben visibly worked through the problem in his head.

"Okay," he concluded at last. "I'll do it. I'll give my notice on Monday when I get back to work. I'll just take the rest of my vacation time and start looking for a new job. But the problem now is that I don't know what I want to do. Hardly another sales job for a shady pharmaceutical company. I really want to *help* people! Not give them a drug they don't need. I'd rather help them take responsibility for their own lives and heal themselves, without drugs. That would be ideal."

Daniel shot him a sidelong glance. "I'm sure you'll find a way, my friend." This was impressive; Ben was really coming around.

~~~

They had made their way back to the apartment when Daniel asked, "Are you ready for our next lesson?"

"Yes, I am. Thank you for reviewing the last one with me. This was big."

"You are such a good student, Ben. It's my pleasure."

"Okay, what's next? Bring it. I'm ready." Ben's eagerness was reflected in his face.

"The next teaching, our seventh lesson, is compassion," Daniel said. He waited for Ben's reaction.
~~~

"Compassion, great. What about it?"

Daniel smiled. "We already touched on this a little last night after the burglary. But there's more to it. First of all, compassion is every human being's true nature. You remember that your soul is divine, right?"

Ben nodded. "I am slowly getting used to that thought."

"Slowly? You're not sold on it yet?" Daniel asked.

"Well, there are things I have done or said that make me feel that I'm not such a great person. I have hurt people or neglected people. When I was eight my goldfish died because I wasn't feeding it. I don't think a divine being would have done something like that. I still feel pretty bad for the goldfish, now that I think about it. And there are other things I did or didn't do as an adult that I feel guilty and ashamed of."

Daniel nodded with sympathy. "Guilt and shame cause you humans great discomfort. They are partly caused by your beliefs that you have not lived up to some self-imposed, higher level of thought and conduct. You basically keep setting yourselves up for failure by inventing very lofty standards of behavior, and then you disappoint yourselves when you don't reach those levels. Your perceived failure creates anger, and even without realizing it, you direct that anger inward. Depression and despair often follow."

"That sounds about right. So how do we prevent it from happening?"

"Learn from the past and let it go. You have all made mistakes in your current lives—and in past lifetimes as well. Clear awareness of your mistakes allows for correction and the intention not to repeat them. But intense guilt, shame, and anger fog your vision and obscure the lessons, which only leads you to repeat the mistakes. And then those negative emotions block your growth and steal your joy. But if you are nonjudgmental about it and are simply aware of your past mistakes, that alone dissolves harmful negativity and helps you learn and not repeat those mistakes in the future."

"I can do that with others more easily than with myself," Ben said thoughtfully. "I wouldn't judge my kid if she had let her goldfish die. Obviously, she wouldn't have been old enough to be responsible for its well-being. A parent should have kept an eye on it. I'm just really hard on myself. Always have been."

"Well, it is easier for most people to have compassion for others than for themselves. How would you show compassion for others—for your daughter, for example?" Daniel inquired.

"I would listen to her, to whatever she wanted to tell me. I used to do that with her. She could always come to me and I would be there for her. She used to love just talking to me and telling me things about school and her friends and what was going on in her life."

"Truly listening is a good way to show compassion, Ben. Patience, and being of service too. Can you think of anything else?"

"Kindness, being caring, being willing to help—"

"Yes, good!" Daniel said.

"I can do that for other people, at least most of the time. But I have a hard time being patient and caring with myself, especially when I perceive myself as failing at something."

"Some of your teachers here on Earth believe that it is useful to see your human failures as tremendous opportunities to learn powerful lessons instead of as reasons for resignation. When you stop pushing away your own humanity in all its darkness and glory, you become more able to embrace other people with compassion. And having compassion for others—even if they are angry, arrogant, selfish, or anything else that you would deem repulsive—means not running from the pain of finding those exact same traits in yourselves. And then you can simply open your heart and find more love and compassion there, for yourselves and your *own* humanity. And from this compassion you will be able to naturally act in service of others. Actions undertaken not from guilt or shame but from the spontaneous outpouring of your hearts."

"So you're saying that if I stop rejecting those negative traits in myself, I can stop rejecting them in others and embrace and have compassion for them no matter what. And out of that I will have more compassion for myself again. It's like a cycle?"

"Yes, it's exactly like a cycle," Daniel agreed. "What you perceive in others is really just a mirror of your own tendencies or traits. So when you notice a repulsive trait in someone else, it reminds you that subconsciously you exhibit the same tendency, and that's why you reject *them* for it."

"Interesting!" Ben tried to wrap his head around it. "And the way out of this is to be aware of it and have compassion for them, and then I will have compassion for myself."

"Correct." Daniel clearly was thoroughly enjoying the conversation. "If you want to take this to a higher level—or a deeper level," he chuckled, "you will find someone right now to practice this on. Who is someone in your life you don't have compassion for? Someone who appears repulsive to you?"

"I can't really think of anyone." Ben was scratching his head. "No one, really."

"Okay, then, how about yourself? What's something that you really don't like about yourself?"

"Does killing the goldfish count?" He was only half joking.

"Of course. Or what about your failure to notice that there was something missing in your marriage and family life—before they left?"

"Yeah … that's a good one," Ben said. That stung.

"Can you have compassion for yourself for that?" Daniel probed.

"Yes, sure. I didn't even know what I wasn't seeing. It's almost like I was numb to it."

"Then maybe you can have compassion for yourself for being numb. You were doing the best you could, given the somewhat low level of consciousness you were operating from at that time." Daniel did his best to say the last piece lightly.

Ben stared at him. "I'm not sure if that was an insult or not."

Daniel smiled. "Well, don't worry. You and about ninety-five percent of your fellow humans are currently still at that low level, acting and reacting like primitive organisms, coming from fear and scarcity, not love and abundance."

"And I guess you could add genetic programming. That's how primitive organisms on this planet function. It's all instinct."

"True," Daniel admitted. "And that's all very useful—for those organisms. But you humans are on the path of evolving now, away from fear, instinct, and automated reflexes and onto a higher level of consciousness. And compassion is one great gateway toward that."

"And you higher beings have mastered that? You're all lovey-dovey and sweet to each other up there?" Ben inquired.

Daniel laughed. "Yes, it's very peaceful and harmonious up there. Hard to explain in human language, given how limited it is. You'll see when you get up there. For now, be grateful that you live in a human body, which is so helpful for this lesson. How would you be able to understand hunger if you had never experienced what hunger feels like in your body? Or cold? How would you know how miserable people are when they are cold if you had never been cold yourself?"

Ben nodded. "I hear you there, my friend. Nothing worse than being cold, hungry, and tired. And if you've ever experienced an extended time of that in your life, you will forever have compassion for every creature that ever has to go through it.

"Hey," Ben added suddenly. "Why don't we find some hungry people and feed them? Are you up for that?"

"Sure!" Daniel jumped to his feet. "But where do we find hungry people?"

"There are usually some homeless people living near the river at this time of the year. Now in the summer they camp out there under the overpass. Let's drive by the store and buy some supplies—food, water, fruits, maybe tooth brushes and soap too." He grabbed his car key and started walking toward the door.

"Good for you, my friend." Daniel smiled kindly. "You just knocked out the entire lesson." He followed him out the door. They went to the grocery store and bought supplies, and for the next two hours they handed them out to the dozen or so homeless people who were living under the overpass.

9. Completion (The Eighth Lesson)

"Lesson number eight. Completion. Ready?" Daniel asked.

"Yeah, man, hit me! I have a feeling this is a big one."

It was Friday and they had spent the day outside, hiking by the river. Daniel really seemed to enjoy the nature on this planet. He had walked from one plant to the next, touching their leaves and seeming to converse with them. He had pointed out birds and butterflies to his human friend, and Ben had noticed how blindly he had been spending his own time, walking around only semi-conscious for most of his life. And there was so much to see, especially in nature. Ants building their hills, bees collecting nectar from flowers—even the grass gently swaying in the breeze seemed to speak of a whole universe of connectedness and belonging.

In nature, everything makes sense, Ben had thought. *Even the most intricate organisms seem to be connected with everything else through an invisible but somehow intelligent network.*

It was late afternoon when they got back to the apartment. Ben gave Daniel a bottle of water and opened a beer for himself. He had been drinking less and less alcohol since meeting Daniel and learning the lessons from him, but occasionally he still fell into his old habit. He had learned another way to relax by now, through meditation, and that didn't just relax him but also cleared his mind immensely. But he doubted he would ever completely forget about a cool, relaxing bottle of beer on a warm summer evening—especially if he felt that he had somehow earned himself a reward.

"Okay. So what is your understanding of the word 'completion'?" Daniel asked.

"Well, when a project is complete and done, signed off on, papers submitted, a renovation finished … I don't know, there are hundreds of examples I could give you."

"Good. In our sense of the meaning," Daniel paused to think for a moment and find the right words, "completion means restoring to fullness. It's a term for removing anything that would drain our power, give us negative emotions, or otherwise be impactful in a negative sense. We call ourselves complete when we have nothing left in us but affection and love for a situation or another person."

"So it's not like closure?" Ben asked.

"Closure is more like closing a door. Having peace, but without creation. Completion, in our sense of the meaning, pertains to completing the past and establishing the space of 'Now what? What's next?' Creation will be possible. If the other person is complete as well, they will be able to create something together. Completion is the canvas for creation. Just as a painter needs a blank canvas to start creating again and paint a new painting, humans need a complete past to create the future. It doesn't work very well to create on top of garbage from the past."

Ben took a sip from his beer. "All right, I think I get it. So what about you? You never told me what happened in your past, what you did to lose your wings, so to speak. What *did* you do?"

Daniel was silent for a moment. When he finally spoke, he sounded distant. "I got involved where I shouldn't have. As angels, we are not allowed to interfere in human affairs. But I just couldn't watch what was happening and not do anything about it. I knew there would be consequences, but at least I helped him."

"Him? Who did you help? What happened?"

"A boy. Maybe seven years old. He was being beaten by his drunken dad. It happened almost every night, and I just couldn't watch it anymore. The boy had called on me for help. I was with him every time. I was just there, comforting him, trying to get his mind off it. And then one night—" He paused.

"What?" asked Ben. He was feeling Daniel's pain. Personally, he would have beaten the crap out of that dad, drunk or not. He had no tolerance for violence, especially toward weaker beings like children or animals. He knew alcoholism was a disease, but there was no excuse to not get help and instead to take it out on one's children. He took another sip from his beer. "Whatever you did, I'm sure he deserved it."

"Well, that's exactly the point," Daniel resumed. "He did *not* deserve it. You humans think that a bad deed shouldn't go unpunished. Fact is, both the boy and his dad were in this situation for a reason. In the bigger picture it made sense."

Ben nearly choked on his beer. "'Sense'? Are you saying it makes *sense* for a drunken father to beat up on his seven-year-old kid?"

"Not here and not now. But in the bigger picture it does. Even if we don't see it and don't understand it. Of course, it's a horrible scenario. But both the father and the son had a reason for being there. It's not a coincidence when those things happen. Do you understand what I'm saying?"

"You're saying that both were in this situation because of their—karma? That they deserved it? Even the seven-year-old?" Ben was appalled. This didn't make sense. A seven-year-old had hardly had the time to rack up that much bad karma in his short life.

"Karma is serious business, my friend. Nothing happens by coincidence. If you didn't arrange for it in this lifetime, then you did in your last. Or in the one before that."

"Okay, I get it. Therefore, my wife leaving me and taking Emily with her was karma," Ben concluded. He killed the last of the beer in one gulp and headed toward the kitchen, hoping there was more in the fridge.

"Nothing happens by coincidence," Daniel repeated when Ben returned. "She probably didn't leave you from one day to the next, did she? In the beginning everything was great, and then things slowly started to change, and nobody did anything about that, and eventually she was fed up and left?"

"How do you know all that? Oh, wait—you were there." Ben couldn't stop himself from sounding derisive. If Daniel was so omnipotent, why didn't he do something to stop things from deteriorating?

Daniel knew exactly what Ben was thinking. "Guides are prohibited from intervening. We can give solace and comfort and whisper in your ears to try to show the right way, but we are not allowed to do more than that. If our signals are too obvious, it could scare humans and that would just backfire."

"Whisper in our ears?"

"Yes." Daniel smiled. "Or did you think that the good and wise thoughts that sometimes help you in your moments of great need are your own?"

Ben shot him an annoyed look. "Well, I thought that occasionally I do have some great ideas myself."

Daniel laughed out loud. It was a kind and innocent laugh. He was so devoid of any negativity, like a big child truly enjoying himself and everything and everyone around him.

"Of course you have good ideas! Especially when you stop thinking, stop paying attention to your obsessive monkey mind for a minute, and start listening to your intuition. Then you have outright excellent thoughts and ideas!"

Ben sighed. "Well, thanks a lot. But let's get back to your story. What did you do to that drunken and miserable dad?"

Daniel turned serious. "I forced him to catch a glimpse of himself. He was holding his kid up by the collar of his pajamas and was ready to strike him. But then he saw himself in the child's wardrobe mirror and nearly dropped him. He couldn't believe what he was seeing. A grown man, so much bigger and stronger than the little boy he was holding up by his neck. And his raised fist. And the fear and hurt in the boy's eyes. And the anger and detachment in his own face. He came to very quickly. His heart nearly broke. He set the boy down carefully, fell on his knees, bowed his head, and cried. He begged his boy for forgiveness. He was so ashamed. He felt like he wanted to die right there and disappear off the face of the Earth. Luckily, the boy was spiritually mature enough to do the right thing—he wrapped his skinny little arms around his father and forgave him right there and then."

"Wow." Ben was astounded. He hadn't expected that, the boy being "spiritually mature." He wasn't sure he would have reacted the same way in that situation.

"Do you understand?" Daniel asked. "The boy did the only thing that made sense to him. He forgave."

"That's really amazing. What a great little kid." Ben paused for a moment. "I still don't understand why you got in trouble for this. It seems to me like you did the right thing."

"I wasn't supposed to get involved. The dad needed to work through his karma on his own time. Humans always have free will, a choice. I didn't give him a choice. I forced him to look at himself when I turned that wardrobe door so he could see himself in the mirror."

"But how is that wrong?" Ben argued.

"Human life is challenging. You are supposed to face your challenges, to learn, grow, and evolve, but only if you choose to. If you choose not to—and that is your right because God gave you free will—we have to respect that and can't interfere. We can't do this difficult work *for* you. It would take away your free will, and it might backfire because you weren't ready. Even if we had the best intentions and it prevented future damage to a person, interference is not allowed."

"Are you saying that there is no such thing as divine intervention? Not legally at least? Legally in angelic terms?"

"Yes, there is. God does it all the time. But we are not God. We don't have the right."

"Okay, so you basically overstepped your boundaries."

"I guess you could put it that way."

"So what happened after that?" Ben asked. "The boy forgave the dad and then what? What happened to you?"

Daniel took a deep breath. "The dad completely turned around that night. He got himself help, he stopped drinking, and he worked every day on improving his relationship with his kid. And with his ex-wife, for that matter. But the council pulled me out. They took my wings from me, literally. They put me in a human body. Do you have any idea how tight it is in here? It's hard to breathe."

Ben raised his eyebrows.

"As angels we don't deal with things like gravity, body weight, tight clothes," Daniel continued. "We are ethereal beings, pure energy."

Ben took a quiet sip from his new beer.

Daniel sighed. "So now I am here, working through and reviewing those lessons so I can go back."

"I still don't understand why helping the guy see what a piece of garbage he was with his kid was so wrong it was actually punishable." Ben spoke very deliberately. "It did help him turn his life around, didn't it? You did a good deed in my eyes. You helped everyone. The guy, the kid, the ex-wife ... who knows who else got spared this guy's anger issues because of what you did? How much *new* bad karma you prevented by doing it?"

Daniel nodded his head. "In this lifetime, here and now, maybe. But it was a violation in the big picture. If I had been human, I could have intervened as much as I wanted to. And I would have, trust me. If I had been there as a human, I would have reacted as any human would, pulled the guy off his kid and possibly applied some form of violence to punish him right there and then. But first of all, think of the consequences. What good would it have done for either one of them in this situation? The kid would have been even more traumatized by watching his dad getting beaten up by some angry stranger."

Ben had to agree with that.

"And then the dad," Daniel continued, "do you honestly think more violence would have gotten through to him? Who knows what he experienced as a kid himself? Probably violence! So how would more violence teach him a lesson? No, he needed the exact opposite. He needed love, compassion, and forgiveness. And self-awareness. Seeing himself in the mirror was exactly what he needed to snap out of his anger spell—and then he experienced his kid's love and forgiveness. It was perfect—"

"And yet," Ben interjected, "you are being *punished* for it. Apparently not that perfect, right?"

"Exactly. I was not there as a human. I had no right to act as a human could have, or to intervene as only God and the highest Masters can. I was supposed to merely comfort the child, who could sense me there, by the way."

"Could he really?" Ben asked, surprised. On the other hand, why not? In a way he had sensed Daniel's existence as well when Daniel was still an angel, not a human. He could feel him next to him on the couch that one time when he was so desperate, and he had seen him vividly in his dreams a couple of times.

"Children are still in touch with their divine nature," Daniel went on. "The older they get, the more they tend to get conditioned by adults to not believe anymore. But at a young age, they are very well aware of their guides—their angels—and the magic that exists in this world."

Ben had a couple of childhood memories himself of being convinced that there was magic on planet Earth. He smiled.

"So, Ben, do you understand the concept of forgiveness?"

"Well, yes, of course I do."

"Great. Is there anyone you still need to forgive in your life?"

"Me?" He wasn't quite sure why he was feeling defensive all of a sudden.

"Well, I don't have anyone, down here or in the higher realms, to forgive for anything," Daniel said. "I forgave myself for intervening in that scenario and for being sent down here. I am complete with all that. So I thought maybe if you had anyone you still needed to forgive, we could learn the lesson through you."

That makes sense, Ben thought. *That's what we've been doing all along anyway.*

"There really isn't anyone," he said. "I forgave Michelle for leaving me a long time ago. I know that I screwed up and that she had been trying to fix it for a while. I just wish I could forgive myself for that."

"Ah, good point!"

Ben looked at Daniel. He was puzzled, and he felt a little annoyed. Why was everything he was working through such a source of joy for this guy?

"Forgive me, my friend. It's just that you are such a good student. You make it so easy for me to review the lessons. And your progress, and my own, makes me happy."

"All right then," Ben grumbled. "I guess we aim to please."

Daniel laughed out loud. "You know that you really don't have to suffer so much, don't you? The pain that you think you are feeling, it's all made up. Are you aware of that?"

Ben thought about that for a moment. The pain he felt when he was thinking about why Michelle had left him felt entirely real to him.

"Just forgive yourself," Daniel urged. "In order to honor God, we accept that our shortcomings are forgiven. Not accepting that doesn't honor God. Imagine a child doing something bad. His father comforts him and forgives him. How would the father feel if the child rejected his forgiveness but insisted on being a bad little boy or girl? The father doesn't want to punish the child, especially if the kid is already upset about his wrongdoing. The child not accepting the father's forgiveness doesn't serve anyone, least of all the child."

Daniel looked at Ben with an air of wisdom. "This is how you have been living your life, Ben, not accepting God's forgiveness. It doesn't honor you and it doesn't honor God."

Ben felt tears dwelling up behind his eyes. His throat felt tight. "God forgave me already?" he managed to say.

"God has never blamed you for anything. In his eyes, there is nothing you can do wrong."

They were quiet then. Ben felt relief wash over him for the first time in months. The tears he cried were tears of joy. He was finally able to forgive himself.

Daniel waited until Ben spoke again. He looked very different now. His face had relaxed so completely that he looked ten years younger. After a while their eyes met.

"Thank you." Ben sounded so serene and peaceful that Daniel couldn't look away. He was moved by his friend's willingness to take on the lessons and to let go of the heavy weight he had been carrying. He sat straighter, and he held his head higher.

"Now that you have forgiven yourself—and you had already forgiven everyone else—are you complete?"

"I believe I am." Ben said with joy.

"Good! Now you can create. What would you like to create?"

"I would like to talk to Michelle and ask *her* for forgiveness. For neglecting them and putting my work above them. And for not being present in the last months and years of our marriage, for being addicted to video games and not witnessing how our daughter was growing up. For not being there. I would like to complete it for *them*."

"Great! And then what do you think could happen? What's your intention?"

"I just want them to be happy. If they're still mad at me, hopefully forgiveness could bring them peace, and then eventually we could start talking again or spending time together, I don't know. I never thought they wanted to see me. Emily has never asked to see me so I just assumed she didn't want to. But I really want to see her! If she's complete, maybe we could start doing some of the things together that we used to do before they left!" His face lit up with recognition and intense joy as he began to realize the whole world of possibility that was slowly developing in his mind.

"You are complete," Daniel smiled.

10. Nothingness (The Ninth Lesson)

It was Saturday. When Daniel got up he found Ben as he had found him for the last few mornings, meditating by himself in the living room.

He quietly put on the kettle and made some tea. After Ben explained to him how the stove worked, he realized he was finding pleasure in such mundane human tasks. He was humming a melody he had picked up somewhere when Ben entered the kitchen, relaxed and smiling.

"Good morning, Daniel. How did you sleep?"

Daniel suppressed a yawn. "Oh, you know. I'm still not used to my human body, but I *am* getting used to the comfortable bed in your spare room." He grinned. "Maybe I'll stick around after we finish my ten lessons."

Ben looked shocked but quickly realized that Daniel was joking. "You've really learned to be funny in a subtle way—are you aware of that?"

Daniel laughed out loud. "Oh, come on, would it be so bad if I stayed?"

Ben thought about it for a moment. "No, of course not. You are almost like my brother by now. But this apartment is too small for so much angelic energy." He grinned.

Now it was Daniel who looked bewildered.

Ben's smile widened. "If you want to stay, you can. But I'll be happy to help you finish your lessons first."

Daniel relaxed. "Okay. I honestly don't know yet what lesson number nine is about. I tried to connect with the Masters and download it last night but it didn't happen. I just feel an urge to go to the city and explore. Do you mind if we do that today?"

"Oh, not at all!" Ben was excited by the idea. "We already covered a lot of nature, and you taught me to connect to the higher realm there. I would love to show you the hustle and bustle of a big city, all the people running around, going shopping, doing errands on a busy Saturday. I hope it won't be too crazy for you, though. There are lots of sounds—noises, really—that you don't find in nature."

"I think I'll be okay with that. I really want to see some human busyness in a city. I imagine it somewhat like a beehive. So should we leave right now?" Daniel was excited too.

"Yes, let's take our teas with us and grab some breakfast downtown—what do you think?"

"Sounds good." Daniel was already on his way to the door.

Like a child, or a puppy about to go for a walk, Ben thought fondly.

~~~

They arrived in the city about an hour later. Ben had thought about the places he wanted to show Daniel: definitely the city center, where the shops and the most people were, the town hall, and the park. Daniel was keen on seeing people in action, and the city center was brimming with them, all seemingly trying to get a week's worth of errands done on a Saturday. Later they could go to the city park to be back in nature and to quiet the mind again.

Daniel took everything in with big, curious eyes. He seemed so innocent sometimes. Ben needed to remind himself that Daniel wasn't really from this planet, that he was much like a tourist—but visiting from a whole other dimension.

They got some breakfast in a popular café and Daniel watched people going in and leaving, some with their breakfast and coffee in hand. Ben had warned him that it was a busy day and some people didn't have time to sit down to eat. But others seemed to do just that. They were meeting their friends for breakfast or lunch and seemed to spend a long time just affectionately talking and laughing and catching up with each other before they went their separate ways again.
~~~

Daniel was fascinated by the multitudes of people he got to observe. They showed up in all shapes and sizes, all ages, in all colors. Some had dogs on leashes, some had brought their children. Most people seemed to be in a good mood as they scurried about running errands, shopping, or meeting someone. Others seemed to have rather grim expressions on their faces. Daniel pointed out a few of these to Ben and asked what he guessed they were thinking about.

"Oh, they're probably just stressed about something. Maybe too many errands to run and not enough time, or not enough money to buy the things they want." Ben shrugged. They were sitting outside overlooking the plaza, and Ben was drinking his second cup of coffee. Daniel had hardly touched his breakfast; he was too distracted by the colorful parade of people.

He was still observing city life when his gaze suddenly went inward. Daniel seemed to be listening to something and Ben could tell by the look on his face that he had made contact with his guides.

When he spoke again, his entire demeanor had changed.

"*Nothingness …*" he uttered. He was ready to tackle his lessons again.

"You talked to your guides?" Ben searched his face for clues. "About … nothingness?"

"Yup, it just downloaded," Daniel said happily.

"Okay, what does it mean?" Ben was curious and ready to move forward as well.

Daniel took a few moments to gather his thoughts. Ben gave him time; he was used to this by now.

"I've been observing these people for a while," he began. "I don't see it as much in the ones who have company with them, their friends or family members. But I see it in everyone who is here by themselves. They are all busy with something in their minds. Have you noticed?"

Ben looked around and studied some of the people who were alone. Some were talking on their phones but those who were not seemed to be thinking about something. They typically gazed down at the pavement with a look of intense focus on their faces. It was almost as though they were listening to something.

"It seems like they are pretty preoccupied with the thoughts in their heads," Ben said. "They look so focused, like they're on a mission or something. Maybe they're just pressed for time, or maybe they have worries and you can see that on their faces."

"It sure looks like it," Daniel confirmed. "They might all have different intents and motivations for being here right now, but what they all have in common is their internal dialogue. They are all listening to their thoughts versus being in the present moment."

"Oh, right, lesson number five," Ben remembered. "Being in the present moment." He hesitated. "You don't think they're present?"

"They are from time to time. After all, they're here to run errands, as you said. Get stuff done. They walk faster and seem in general more intentional in their behavior than the people who are here with their friends or family and are just leisurely enjoying the moment and their time together."

"What are you getting at?" Ben wasn't sure he followed.

"You humans have about sixty thousand recurring thoughts in your head every day, most of which are redundant, repetitive, negative thoughts. Those thoughts start when you first get up in the morning—have you noticed that? What is the first thing that crosses your mind when you get up in the morning?"

"Well, let's see," Ben started. "Sometimes it's 'I don't want to get up yet.' That's when I'm still tired. Or 'I have so much work to do today. I don't know if I can get it all done.' Lately I haven't had those thoughts, though. I've been happy to get up and meditate early, and I've felt good and hopeful in the mornings. But before you got here ..." He stopped and looked at Daniel. It had only been a week since his angel friend had "fallen from the sky" but it seemed like eternity. "Before you got here I was stuck in a never-ending cycle of negative thinking. All day long I would worry either about work, our faulty product, or my impending divorce. Mostly what I thought about was Michelle and Emily and how I was going to make it through the day."

"Most people are like that," Daniel nodded. "Their minds start churning early in the morning or sometimes even at night! A lot of people wake up at night and worry about things they have no control over in that moment. And then they have a hard time going back to sleep. The next morning they worry even more, adding to their list fretting about lost sleep and being tired and their face looking puffy ..."

Ben grinned. "That can be a whole world of worry in itself for some people. A puffy face."

Daniel looked at him with a raised eyebrow. "You have never done that, of course."

"Worry about my natural beauty? Of course not!" They both laughed.

"Okay, so where are we going with this?" Ben was eager to move on.

"Some of your earthly cultures are well aware of the state of mind where there are no thoughts present. Your Buddhists call it *Sunyata*. It's the state of mind we refer to as 'Nothingness.' And it's the only space we can truly create from. Otherwise we would be creating on top of something else—existing thoughts, worries, or concepts—and that's not true creation. It's only adding on. Make sense?"

"Yes. I've been there occasionally in some of my most recent meditations. It felt like my mind was completely empty. It was hugely relaxing."

"Right!" Daniel exclaimed. "And that's where we want to be most of the time, but humans hardly ever are. They entertain thoughts and worries, their internal dialog, all day long."

"And sometimes at night," Ben added.

"Correct! Thanks for paying attention."

Ben was trying to remember something that tugged at the edge of his memory. "I think I read an article a little while ago about something like that. The Dalai Lama said in an interview that a quiet mind leads to enlightenment. Is that correct? I never really grasped it at that time. What is he saying? By the way, do you know who the Dalai Lama is?"

"Sure," Daniel said. "He is one of the most magnificent Masters. He chose to come down here into human form again to help others. He is very beloved by many on your planet Earth and in the higher dimensions as well."

Ben simply looked at his friend, speechless.

When words returned, Ben said, "Okay, then. So you *both* are saying that we should stop the brain chatter and focus on emptiness in the mind?"

"When we are free from attachment to all outer objects, the mind will be in peace. Our essence of mind is intrinsically pure, and the reason why we are perturbed is that we allow ourselves to be carried away by the circumstances we are in. If you are able to keep your mind unperturbed, unattached to circumstances, you will be able to attain enlightenment."

That definitely sounds like something the Dalai Lama would say, Ben thought.

"That place of stillness in the mind is the only space where you can find true inspiration and true creation. You need to realize that this entire world you have created around yourself is an illusion. Many of your earthly cultures talk about that as well. You humans tend to add meaning to absolutely everything that happens around you. Everything that you observe or that happens to you—or doesn't happen to you—is judged and will be labeled with a meaning. Most of the time, this happens entirely subconsciously and is tinged by experiences, judgments, and decisions from your past."

"Whoa!" Ben said.

"None of this is real, Ben." Daniel repeated.

"None of what, this city, the people?"

"None of the meanings you are adding to everything. There is no significance to anything that happens around you. *You* are the center of your own universe and *you* add the meanings that create this tapestry of your own world. The city and the people are real in the present moment. They move, they walk, they go about their business. But the *meanings* you are adding to everything—are not. Just watch. Watch that couple over there."

A young couple had sat down a few tables over. Ben hadn't noticed them while they were drinking their coffees but they seemed to be arguing now. He focused on their voices and was able to make out their conversation.

"I can't believe you were late again," she was saying somewhat sulkily.

"I'm sorry, babe. I tried to be here on time."

That didn't sound exactly cheerful, Ben thought. *Poor guy.* He felt for him. Nothing worse than a male bad conscience and the feeling that you can never get it right for her.

"The problem is, you're always late!"

"Jeez, honey! I was working!" The man was clearly feeling defensive now, and lashing out at her. "Can't you hang out by yourself for a few minutes? Play with your phone or something?"

"I could, of course, but why do you say ten when you mean ten forty-five? Am I not worth your time? I really don't think that you respect me very much. Do you even love me?"

She sounds like she's about to cry. Ben cringed. *Oh no, no tears, please. That's the worst.*

The man—husband?—was getting even more frustrated now, and Ben didn't have to strain anymore to hear.

"You're always so negative. I can never do anything right for you. I was working on a Saturday for *us*! You want the nice house and your nice things, don't you?"

Then the couple got up and left the cafe, still arguing.

He sounds hurt under all that anger, Ben observed. *He probably works his butt off to afford her a certain lifestyle—and she doesn't appreciate him for it. Bummer … they otherwise seem like a nice couple. I wonder how long they've been married.*

"What did you observe?" Daniel interrupted Ben's thought process with a smile.

"Well, they both seem to be hurt and not feeling appreciated by the other. I think with some good communication they could solve all that pretty quickly, but it almost looked like they were trapped in their past."

"What do you mean?" Daniel encouraged.

"They said 'you always' or 'you never'—do this and that. Sounds like an old script."

"You're right!" Daniel was beaming that happy smile he always wore when Ben was being a "good student."

"Most of their fears and worries come from their past, probably their childhoods. The events that led to their current misconceptions of reality are obscured now and buried deep in their respective subconscious minds."

"What does that have to do with Nothingness?" Ben inquired.

"You can only reach Nothingness through the awareness of your constant thoughts and meaning making. They were both adding meaning to things that were happening—or not happening. His being late made her think that—"

"That he doesn't respect her," Ben interrupted. "She asked him if he even loved her!"

"Correct," Daniel was so excited he seemed to be on fire. "And what was the meaning that *he* added?"

"He seemed to feel unappreciated for working so hard so that they can live in a nice house and afford nice things. He works hard for *them*, not for himself, and she doesn't seem to see that."

"That was his interpretation, yes?" Daniel asked.

"Yes, that's what it seemed like."

"Now notice how much meaning *you*'ve been adding to their argument," Daniel said. "All your interpretations and assessments about their conversation and what happened and their lifestyle, those were also nothing more than meanings that you added."

"Huh." Ben was dumbfounded. He hadn't noticed he was doing that. "I guess I was."

"Now Nothingness is the opposite of that. We don't add meaning. We might observe people and situations and what's happening in the present moment, but we are very much aware that whatever happens doesn't *mean* anything. In fact, *nothing* that happens—or doesn't happen—means anything. It only has meaning if we *give* it meaning."

Ben reflected on this. "Nothing means anything?"

"Only the meaning you give it. And of course, you have options. You can give things a positive or a negative meaning. But most of the time you're on autopilot and all your past experiences, assessments, and evaluations take over for you and hand out meanings subconsciously and automatically. And they're not always positive."

Ben took a moment to think about this, looking around at their surroundings.

"We all do this, all the time. Correct?" He looked back at Daniel.

"Correct."

"And if we didn't add our own personal meanings to everything around us all the time? We would just observe but not add anything on to it?"

"Then you would realize that 'This is it.' Right now, and it doesn't mean anything. It is not significant. There would be no attachment to circumstances, the mind would be unperturbed and quiet—*Nothingness*—and that would lead to enlightenment."

"And all I have to do is to just observe and not add meaning."

"Correct."

They fell quiet then and simply watched the people around them. Somewhere, a dog barked. An ambulance drove past with its siren howling. Ben noticed it but didn't think anything of it. A lady spilled the contents of her purse while rummaging through it looking for something. Ben watched her kneel down and pick up the items off the street. He briefly thought he should help her but then he saw another woman approach and bend down to help. He watched them exchange a few friendly words before they parted and walked on. He saw a kid on a skateboard nearly get wiped out by a truck backing slowly out of a delivery alley. Luckily the kid was able to swerve around the truck. Life just went on, and the constant flow of little events seemed to take on its own rhythm. Ben found himself relaxing in the middle of all of this. He noticed people talking, laughing, even arguing, and managed to simply observe without adding any meaning or significance to any of it at all. His mind became still. He looked over toward Daniel and their eyes met.

Daniel saw it immediately. In the middle of a busy city day, amid people running errands and going about their business,

Ben had found complete stillness. He was fully present, his mind was quiet, and he was ready for the next and final lesson.

11. Surrendering to a Higher Power (The Final Lesson)

The next morning, Sunday, Ben and Daniel were sitting on the living room floor, quietly sipping their tea, feeling peaceful and comfortable after their morning meditation.

"We only have one lesson left, correct?" Ben asked lazily.

"Yeah. Amazing."

"Any idea what it is yet?"

"No. We should go outside, get some rays and move our bodies around."

"Park? River?"

"Let's go to the river. I have grown quiet fond of the nature there."

They grabbed more tea and some apples and headed toward the river reserve.

~~~

"Why don't you sign the divorce papers, Ben? Why can't you let her go?" They had chosen a spot in the shade of an old willow tree that hugged the riverbank. Daniel was chewing on a
~~~

piece of apple and looked entirely relaxed and content with himself.

"It's not that easy," Ben began hesitantly. "I don't know why I'm having such a hard time with it. I wonder if she's seeing anyone new. She might not be, but I haven't asked her. I kind of really don't want to hear that she's madly in love with some new guy." He paused.

"I've looked at this from all different angles," he continued. "Would she be better off without me? Or should I convince her that I'm still the *one* for her? I know that I screwed up."

"How did you screw up? Remind me." Daniel seemed unimpressed with Ben's world of story and pain. He was watching some little fish as they quickly dashed back and forth in the clear, shallow water below them.

"I lost my job. I became a slob. I was playing video games for hours. I didn't spend enough time with my family. It's all my fault. I pushed them away."

"Remember calling your boss and cleaning up with him about your cutting corners at work?"

"Lesson number four, truth in word and deed. Yes, that was great. He was thrilled that I came forward like that. Why are you asking?"

"I think you should call Michelle and talk to her. Tell her that you've changed, that you have taken responsibility for your life since you've been apart, and that you are available to be a better partner and father now."

"I did that last night. I called her and told her all of that. It was right after we came back from the city and I was still in that space of Nothingness. I thought if I didn't add meaning to anything she said, it wouldn't hurt so much if she didn't want me back."

"What did she say?" Daniel's expression said, *"Why didn't you tell me?"*

Ben didn't seem to see it. "Not much. She mostly listened. I told her that I am really cleaning up my life and I'm aware that I wasn't fully there for them. And that I have changed and want to give it another try. In my opinion, I'm a different person now. And especially since you showed up in my life, I've changed my views on so many things. But she didn't say anything. She only thanked me for calling her and wished me good luck with everything. And then we hung up." His face was clouded with grief.

"I don't know what to think anymore. But I just can't let her go. It would be like tearing out a piece of my heart—and throwing it away."

Daniel looked at him with sadness. His voice was filled with compassion when he spoke.

"Letting go is not like closing the door on people. It's more like taking a weight off them. Think of them as birds trying to fly but with a weight tethering them to the ground. If we release them—remove that weight—they will feel much better and they will fly. And sometimes instead of flying away, they fly in big circles. And once they've enjoyed their freedom for a while, they realize that they're missing something. And then they come back to us."

Ben looked skeptical. "You think she would come back if I let her go?"

"If it's meant to be, dear friend. Sometimes the people in our lives are only meant to be with us for a little while to help us learn a teaching, or to comfort or accompany us. And sometimes—especially when we're with a true soul connection—this connection lasts for a lifetime and beyond. But sometimes even our true soul mates need to venture out on their own for a little while to explore themselves and their capabilities and to learn teachings that they alone were meant to learn. Especially if they have always been with someone and never really spent time alone, they often don't feel like they have a sense of who they are. They want to create an identity for themselves. But that doesn't mean that they won't ever return and want to create a union again."

"I guess I'm having a hard time seeing that, Daniel. I feel like she got tired of me completely and once she was gone she realized how happy she is on her own. And maybe now she's already with someone new and she simply stopped loving me."

"Sometimes their desire to venture out on their own has nothing to do with the one who was left behind. Sometimes it isn't personal at all. They simply need space to find themselves, or to reinvent themselves, or even just to spend some time alone. Humans are funny this way—they want the union and are afraid of being alone, but they also want to keep their sense of individuality, and—"

"I do take it personally, though," Ben interrupted. "I take it hugely personally. How am I supposed to just forget about it, forget about what we had? If her leaving me isn't personal, I don't know what is."

They both fell silent.

After a while Ben started to feel more at peace again. He took a few deep breaths and watched the little fish that Daniel was so fascinated with. He became present in the moment and realized that again he had been adding a whole lot of meaning, which in turn led to feelings of pain and grief. He came back to Nothingness and relaxed.

"Good job," Daniel acknowledged, nodding and smiling. He had just been sitting there, watching Ben patiently, waiting for him to take the next step. "You found peace again. Now what?"

Ben knew in his heart that he needed to make a decision. Maybe it was time to trust and listen to his guide's advice again. Because that, he realized, was what Daniel had been for him this whole time—his guide.

He sighed. "I'm not sure. What do you suggest, angel?" He looked at his friend.

Daniel's voice was firm. "Let her go. And have faith that it's the right thing to do."

"Sign the divorce papers?"

"Yes, and forgive yourself. You did the best you could with what you had at that time, on the level that you were on. It's not your fault. This was meant to be—you were led to learn something and you did. Forgive yourself for not being able to give her what she needed at that time, with what she had, on the level that *she* was on."

Slowly, Daniel's words started to sink in. Ben felt a wave of emotions wash over him. "I loved her so much that I did all the wrong things. I was so attached to her, to our marriage, that I didn't see what she really needed. I was hiding. I thought I couldn't live up to it anyway. I just wanted it to be like it was in the beginning when everything was easy."

"Forgive yourself for that. And tell her. Let her know that you are letting her go."

When Daniel finished speaking, he tilted his head. He was listening inwardly again.

"They want me to tell you something," he continued. "*You are a child of God and you are godless if you do not know that, believe that, and act like it. Everything,* everything, *is designed to support you. God wants you to prove to him that you know that. That you have faith, that you trust, and that you will take that step."*

They were silent for a while. Ben needed a moment to digest what he'd just heard—and to give his skin time to stop tingling.

"That's pretty heavy," he eventually said. "So this lesson is about what, faith?"

"Faith is part of it, but it's more than that," Daniel continued. "The lesson is about surrendering your personal will to a higher power and trusting that you will come out a better version of yourself. Surrendering like that initiates a sacred shift of perspective. It helps you shift your obsession with your sometimes very small, individual concerns, which cause so much of your mind's distraction and make you feel separated from *Source*. Surrendering increases your awareness that there is a bigger picture, that a higher power is driving all of this, and that your life has been preplanned from the start, guided by divine love from the beginning."

"All of this was preplanned?"

Daniel grinned from ear to ear. "You thought your life was just a coincidence?"

"I just can't imagine the vastness of a being or an intelligence that would be able to orchestrate all of our lives like this.

How much planning and effort that would take!" He looked pointedly at Daniel.

While Daniel was still obviously enjoying their conversation, he became more solemn now. In fact, Ben noticed that he had started emanating a soft glow again. A subtle light seemed to be radiating outward from his body. It was slightly pulsating, as though it was coming and going, and it was all around him—as well as inside him.

"You will have to let her go," Daniel continued. "Completely unselfishly, with no attachment to any outcome, just for the sake of faith, hope, and love. She has free will. Let her choose whether she wants to be with you or not. Complete this for her. Give her the space to create something new with you if she chooses to."

"Completion—lesson number eight." Ben muttered. "It's all coming together now, isn't it?"

"This is our final test, my friend. Can you have faith, surrender your own personal will to a higher power, and let her go?"

"So if I let my wife go and give her the divorce she desires, *you* will pass your final test?" Ben was avoiding the question. "Why is that?"

"I have nothing to let go of," Daniel shrugged. "There is no sacrifice I could make to prove that I have faith in the higher power. I know what it's like up there. I *have* a relationship with God. This isn't about me."

"This is about *me?*" Ben was shocked. *When did I start playing such a big role in these lessons?*

Daniel's light had expanded. While still subtle, it seemed to completely engulf him now as he sat there under the willow tree on the riverbank.

"Daniel, you're … glowing." Ben said it slowly and with awe.

"I feel lighter in this body now. It's almost like I could lift off and fly. But we're not done here."

"If I let go of Michelle, sign the divorce papers, and declare her and me "complete," you will—leave and go back to where you came from?" He looked up to the sky. His mind didn't want to believe what was happening but his eyes weren't betraying him. He was noticing that Daniel's light seemed to be growing brighter by the minute.

"We have to pass the final test. This test is yours alone, Ben—it's up to you now. But you and I are *one*. When you have a relationship with God, with *oneness*, nothing possesses essential, enduring identity because everything is interconnected and in constant flow. God is beyond one form yet expressed through all forms. If you learn the lesson well and pass it, I will too."

"It's all on me now." Ben said.

"No pressure," Daniel grinned. His personality hadn't changed much, despite that fact that he was now radiating light. Ben couldn't stop looking at him. The glow emanating from him was of a beautiful, transparent white light. It seemed to be flowing—or pulsating—at a high vibration, emitting a feeling of complete acceptance and love. Daniel seemed unimpressed with it, as though it was a normal state for him to find himself in.

Ben was suddenly overcome with curiosity. "So up there," he pointed to the sky, "do you all glow like that?"

Daniel laughed. "We are pure energy, my friend. Yes, we do."

"That must be really beautiful ..." Ben muttered. He felt a yearning to go with Daniel. His heart grew heavy at the thought of his leaving.

"Ben, it's okay." Daniel knew what his human friend was feeling. "I will always be around—you just call on me and I'll be there. You are not alone. And when the time comes and it's your turn to leave your body, I will come down here and pick you up." He smiled.

"That's really nice of you. Thank you." Ben had never thought about his own death or dying, but the prospect of being "picked up" by an angelic friend was definitely comforting.

He cleared his throat and got back to business. "We'd better make sure we get you back up there. So, I didn't bring the darn divorce papers but when we get back to the apartment I will sign them and send them off."

"Are you sure?" Daniel asked. "Don't just sign them because you want to get rid of me." He let out a hearty laugh.

Ben frowned at him briefly but then explained. "No, I want to. I want to surrender my own personal will to the higher power that makes you glow like this. I understand now that there is a whole realm up there—dimensions that are ruled by an infinite, loving intelligence that knows all of our whereabouts at all times and keeps orchestrating our lives to the most intricate detail. All so we can learn to be better beings every day. I can't even imagine how much brain power and exabytes it must take to be so aware of everything!" He shook his head. "I am ready to surrender this whole divorce issue to them. They seem to know infinitely more than I do and what is best for everyone. I hope that things with Michelle and me will turn around, but at this point … maybe we aren't meant to be together anymore. Maybe this is all happening for a very good reason, and I want to be part of the solution, not the problem."

Daniel looked at Ben proudly, and fondly. "I think you've got, it my friend."

"There is also the matter of letting *you* go," Ben continued sadly. "I surrender that to the higher power as well. I would be happy if you would get your wings back and make it back to …" He pointed skyward again. "Heaven or whatever you call that place. Nothing would please me more. But I am sad to let you go, and now I'm actually jealous and can't wait to get up there myself. *If* they will have me."

"Of course they will! There are souls up there that are already looking forward to reuniting with you! But I think now is not your time."

"Okay, then," Ben sighed. "Is that it? Or are they waiting for me to physically sign the divorce papers to let you back? What else do we have to do?"

"I don't know. Let me tune in with them."

They both returned their attention to the little fish that were still gathering in the shallow water in the shade of the willow. Ben thought about how he had changed in these last few days with Daniel. He had so much more peace now! He had made the decision to quit the job that had caused him so much worry lately. He knew in his heart that his days of selling pharmaceuticals were over. He wanted to do something meaningful that would really help others, and that would forward the evolution of humanity on planet Earth.

He also thought about Michelle and Emily—and felt a lightness in his heart that he couldn't rationally explain. Now that he had made the decision to sign the divorce papers and end his marriage, he felt confident that things would work out to the highest and best for all of them. If it was meant to be, they would find a way back to each other. He felt a oneness with everyone and everything that he had missed his whole life, and had now found.

Yet as he thought of Daniel leaving, his heart hurt and he felt his throat constricting. He still couldn't believe he had spent so much time with an actual angel! But just one glance at his friend, deep in meditation and surrounded by a white, shimmering light, helped confirm the reality of the situation. This week had not been a dream. It was as real as the ground they were sitting on and the water flowing calmly past their feet. He admired the glow surrounding Daniel. He wondered if he would have a glow like that when he left his body and became just a soul again.

Daniel looked up and their eyes met. For a while neither one of them spoke, but Ben felt that Daniel was ready to leave. Even his eyes were lighter, seeming almost transparent.

"Now this is interesting," Daniel began slowly.

Ben looked at him expectantly.

"I connected with my guides. We passed the ten tests. I can go back now." He smiled.

Ben's heart leapt with joy for his friend. "Excellent! I never thought you wouldn't, but now that we have confirmation I am so relieved and happy for you! When are you leaving?" This was such a funny sensation in his heart—he was ecstatic for Daniel, but now deep sadness was also setting in.

"I will leave soon," Daniel said. He looked up at the sky and then at a spot next to him. "My guides are already here."

"They're picking you up? That's nice," Ben said. He couldn't see anyone but he had no doubt that the beings were there.

"Ben!" Daniel exclaimed. "They're telling me that you can come!" His luminous face was beaming. "You passed the ten tests as well as I did. And you did the final lesson for both of us. You have earned your wings. You can come with me … if you want to."

"What? They're inviting me to heaven? Now?" Ben was overwhelmed. He felt such honor, and joy. He could almost *feel* the love emanating from the beings around Daniel although he couldn't see them. Daniel's light was shining brightly now, with pure energy and love.

And suddenly, Ben knew what he would do. He felt his heart break as he spoke his next words. "I'm sorry, my friend. But it's not my time. I have work to do here now. I want to help other people find the peace and understanding that I have found through you."

Daniel nodded. "I know, Ben. And you will be an amazing teacher."

They shared a long moment sitting on the riverbank and enjoying each other's company one last time. Words were not needed to convey the love and connection between them.

Eventually Ben started gathering his things. "I think we should head home. Are you coming?"

"No, Ben," Daniel said slowly. "I will stay here. You go and sign the divorce papers and send them off. Talk to Michelle in a few days and make sure that she got them. Tell her what you experienced."

"I will do that." Ben stood and shouldered his daypack. "Are you sure you're not coming?"

Daniel laughed his quiet, good-natured laugh. "It's time for me to go now."

Ben felt tears burning behind his eyes. The realization that this was it was sinking in. Daniel was leaving. He was going back to heaven!

"It's okay, Ben," Daniel said gently. "We were hoping this moment would come. We were both working toward it. I need to go back now. And as I said, you can come with me if you want."

"I want to. Believe me, I really do. But it's not time for me yet. I need to stay."

"Then so long, my friend. Call on me any time you need some support down here. I'll be there for you."

Ben turned and started walking toward the parking lot. He didn't want Daniel to see him cry. He was so happy for him!

When he looked back, Daniel was gone.

~~~

Back at the apartment, the first thing Ben did was to take out the divorce papers and sign them in all the places Michelle had marked for him. He didn't even read the papers. He stuffed them into an envelope, addressed it to Michelle, and carried it outside, back to his car. He would drive to the post office and make sure the envelope got the correct amount of postage to reach Michelle in the next few days.

His heart felt light. His eyes hadn't stopped searching the sky for his friend, but he was sure Daniel was busy doing other things, like catching up with his old angel friends. Ben laughed softly at the thought of that.

As he was walking to the parking lot, a car pulled up beside him. A window rolled down and a familiar face smiled warmly at him.

"Michelle?" His heart skipped a beat. He didn't want to trust his eyes.

She stopped the engine and got out of the car with familiar grace. She was wearing the jeans he liked and his favorite top. She walked up to him, put her arms around him, and pulled him close.
~~~

THE END

AFTERWORD

I didn't grow up believing in angels. As a young child I used to pray to Jesus before bed but that was the extend of mine or my family's interest in religion. We went to church on Christmas and Easter and that was about it.

I grew up being interested in animals and nature. I spent most of my free time outdoors, watching birds or trying to track animals in the forest. I studied Biology and Biological Sciences and went to work at a research institute in Germany doing laboratory research. I used to think that I have an analytical mind and angels were just something I personally didn't believe in. Others around me did but I couldn't relate to their inclinations.

And then I saw an angel! It was so unexpected and my mind was so unprepared for it - and it was one of the strangest and most impactful experiences of my life to date. I still remember exactly every detail of that encounter and what the angel looked like. I was flying from Germany to San Diego with a layover in Philadelphia. During my layover there was a thunderstorm but it had passed by the time we boarded our connecting flight. We took off in the sunshine and flew around a massive thunder cloud - and I saw a gigantic "angel" standing there in a crevice in the cloud. He was looking directly at me (the plane/us) but no-one else seemed to notice him. He looked like a marble statue, with long folded wings, a beautiful, peaceful face and he was smiling! I rubbed my eyes, looked away and out the window again multiple times, and he was still there. I noticed that while we were flying around the cloud (and him) that his head had started to turn with us. His body was still facing forward but his head and gaze were following us/the plane. The whole time he seemed to be looking directly into my eyes, smiling. I couldn't believe it and my mind was running wild. Eventually I elbowed my seat neighbor and almost yelled at the poor woman, "Look out the window! There's Jesus!" She looked out for a while and then looked at me, smiling mildly (I thought she was going to pat my head). She didn't see him and when I looked out the window again he was gone. The thunder cloud was unchanged, the crevice was still there, but the angel was gone.

This whole encounter deeply disturbed me and shook all my rational, scientific beliefs to the core. It opened my mind though, and I soon started searching for another truth beside our conventional, materialistic one. And now, 17 years later, after many teachings and some more, surprising and beautiful experiences I am clear that the truth I have started to find, that higher awareness and the connection to higher guides and higher realms, has brought me so much more peace and understanding - of the bigger picture and the benevolence and lawfulness that God/the Universe is - than I could have ever wished for.

I named my angel Daniel. I'm not sure where that name came from but I believe that I heard it when I saw him in that Philadelphia thunder cloud. I started feeling his presence - and other guides' as well - around me after that encounter, especially after I started my spiritual journey and when I actively call on him. I studied yoga and became an instructor and during most of my meditations I can feel their presence.

Daniel "helped" me write this book. I believe that I partly channeled him and that he dictated most of his teachings to me and I simply wrote them down. I still appreciate science, facts and evidence… but I'm aware that our science and scientific equipment simply aren't at that point yet where we can "prove" the existence of angels, guides and other dimensions. For now, we'll just have to go with that feeling in our hearts when we simply know that something is the truth, as unbelievable as it may occur.

My deepest wish is that more of humanity will see those signs from "Heaven" and will know that we are taken care of at all times, no matter our circumstances.

With love,

Corry Lang

ACKNOWLEDGMENTS

To everyone who helped create this book, in this dimension and the others.

I am blessed to be surrounded by so many amazing people whose support and insights have been so encouraging and helped me to write this book.

My heartfelt thanks to my editor Sheridan McCarthy who helped me with my written English and managed to keep me on track for as long as it took to finish the manuscript. Her humor, openness and insights made it an exquisite pleasure to work with her and I can only recommend her.

Thank you Prudence Makhura for the wonderful cover design.

I am full of love and appreciation for the special people in my life whose uplifting love, friendships, feedback and general support helped me through the writing and publishing process: Mark Shapiro, Claudia Seifert, Allison Burgueno, Celine Maury, Shannon Ward, Damon Kinnaman, Linda Bodiker, Adam Turner, Andrea Harris, Maya Naik, Omar Mendez, Luis Leon and Laura Converse.

Much love to my parents Gisela and Siegfried Lang who always love and support me and who really encouraged me to write this book.

About the Author

Corry Lang is a certified yoga teacher, life and emotional health coach and nutritional detox consultant who lives in Encinitas, California. Originally from Germany where she had worked in scientific research labs for a number of years, she moved to San Diego in 2002 for a fresh start. She wrote "Closer to Heaven" to capture her own method of coaching after she witnessed how her clients successfully transformed their lives with those simple yet profound ontological and yogic principles.

COMING SOON

Closer to Heaven the Workbook

In this practical and easy to use workbook you will get to practice and apply all the lessons that Daniel taught Ben.

Please visit **www.CorryLangCloser.com** for "Closer to Heaven the workbook" (release date: Summer 2019) as well as the e-book version of "Closer to Heaven - Ten Principles to grow your wings and create Heaven on Earth" and any book updates!

Please join my e-mail list for updates, a free monthly newsletter and frequent specials at **www.CorryLang.com.**